jazz singers

consultant editor: paul roland

introduction by: roy carr

jazz singers

First published in 1999 by Hamlyn an imprint of Octopus Publishing Group Limited, 2–4 Heron Quays, London, E14 4JP

© Octopus Publishing Group Limited 1999
Interview text copyright © contributor/magazine/IPC Magazines Ltd.

Executive Editor Mike Evans
Creative Director Keith Martin
Executive Art Editor Geoff Fennell
Picture Research Zoë Holtermann
Production Controller Joanna Walker

Consultant Editor Paul Roland

First published in the United States in 2000 by Billboard Books, an imprint of Watson-Guptill Publications, a division of BPI Communications, Inc., at 1515 Broadway, New York, NY 10036

Library of Congress Cataloging-in-Publication Data for this title can be obtained from the Library of Congress.

Library of Congress Card Number: 99-068331

ISBN: 0-8230-8342-X

Produced by Toppan Printing Co Ltd

Printed in China

First printing 2000

1 2 3 4 5 6 7 8 9 / 08 07 06 05 04 03 02 01 00

contents

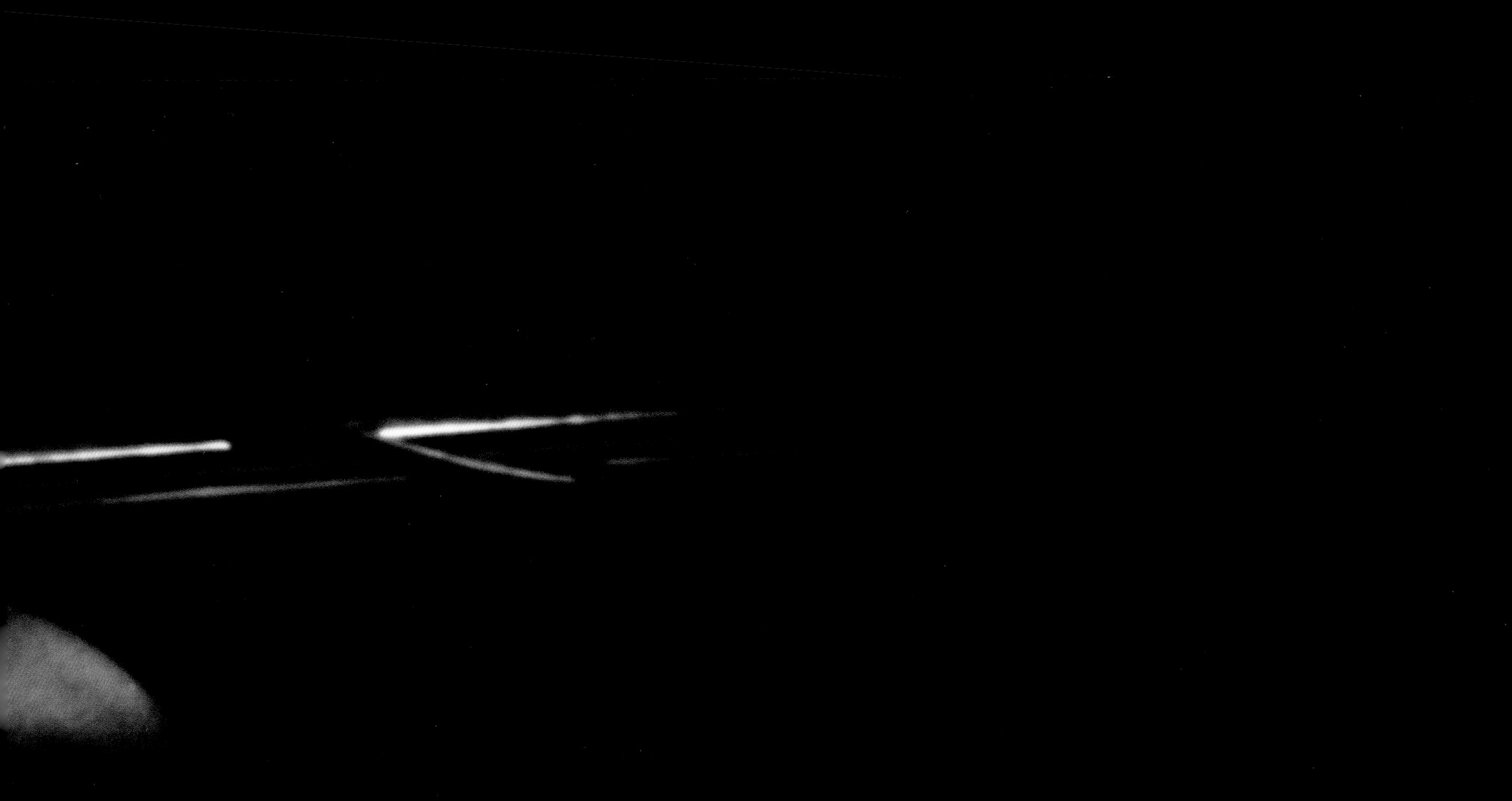

In this MTV-dominated era of rapidly-diminishing attention spans, it may be quite difficult to comprehend that there was a time when the *Melody Maker*'s editorial policy was devoted almost entirely to jazz musicians, and to those singers whose style ranged from the uncompromising full-on stance of bebop-babbling Babs Gonzales, to the celebratory expertise of American Song Book interpreters such as Tony Bennett—singers who possessed the forethought to constantly surround themselves with the very best available jazz players.

Although *Melody Maker* has documented an ever-changing musical scenario for close on eight successive decades, it was from the mid-1940s—when jazz was still very much the popular music of the day—right on past the years of Beatlemania, that tens of thousands of its readers enjoyed a weekly intake of the very latest one-night-stand adventures in the world of big bands and celebrity vocalists.

In those frantic years immediately following World War II, when almost all US-published fan magazines were an extension of a publicist's office, the London-based *Melody Maker* attracted writers such as Leonard Feather and Max Jones—just two of a small coterie of knowing observers who helped pioneer the kind of in-depth music press reportage that is now taken for granted.

Sure, most artists employed one or more fixed-grin press agents to buff up their public profile (or defuse any possible scandals resulting from private indiscretions), but, in retrospect, it can be seen that journalists had more accessibility and, with few exceptions, situations weren't nearly as orchestrated as they are today.

Whereas there were those who concerned themselves with nothing more than banalities, the likes of Feather and Jones seized the moment to file accurate insights.

They didn't betray such trust, and in some instances they became confidants of a number of the artists they interviewed, most notably, in Max Jones's case, Billie Holiday.

It needs to be established that the highly respected American periodicals *Downbeat* and *Metronome* had also meticulously documented the scene over the years, but *Melody Maker's* uniqueness was its then unrivaled position as a weekly tabloid music newspaper, and the fact that it could react to a story as it broke. Such immediacy didn't pass unnoticed.

Even before Billie Holiday made her first recordings, *Melody Maker* was running copy on her at the instigation of her champion and future producer, John Hammond. Much of the *Maker's* loyal support may have come about as a result of its extensive coverage of the local dance band circuit, but it was the instant excitement and Hollywood-style glamour associated with the seemingly larger-than-life American performers that frequently attracted front-page banner headlines. Who wouldn't be impressed by sharp-suited personalties who answered to the names of Count, Duke, Zoot, Dizzy, Mr B, Slim, Illinois, Flip, Prez, or Buddy?

In the case of the singers, the majority had come up through the ranks of the big swing bands, having been promoted from a "with vocal refrain" credit on a record label to solo star billing. In the process, a select few had the distinction of being affectionately referred to by such monikers as "The Voice" (Frank Sinatra), "The Velvet Fog," (Mel Tormé), "The Divine" Sarah Vaughan), and "Queen of the Blues" (Dinah Washington).

Big bands were boot camp for aspiring crooners and songbirds—an uncompromising hard-knocks environment that enforced strict disciplines and, initially, few rewards. For the most part, the featured singers were on the payroll as a decorative distraction between showcasing the more highly paid star sidemen. It was inevitable that being in such close proximity to so many great instrumentalists rubbed off. The strongest survived, the remainder slipped back into the small town obscurity from which they had briefly emerged.

Few big bands had the instrumental signature sound of a Basie, Ellington, Goodman, or Kenton and, ironically, it was often the featured vocalists who supplied a band's all-important instant identification to the point where they eventually upstaged all else.

Included among those singers who stayed the course to graduate with honors (and who are featured in this volume) were June Christy (Stan Kenton), Ella Fitzgerald (Chick Webb/Dizzy Gillespie), Billie Holiday (Count Basie/Artie Shaw), Peggy Lee (Benny Goodman), Anita O'Day (Gene Krupa/Stan Kenton), Sarah Vaughan (Earl Hines/Billy Eckstine), and Dinah Washington (Lionel Hampton), while, for a time, Louis Armstrong and Billy Eckstine (trumpet players both) fronted their own ill-fated cash-guzzling big bands—in the case of Mr B, a veritable bebop crucible that featured Bird, Diz, Dexter, and a whole hoard of zoot-suited hombres.

Feted for her vocalese version of tenorman Wardell Gray's "Twisted," British expatriate Annie Ross went that extra mile when she successfully teamed up with vocal bop meisters Dave Lambert and Jon Hendricks, who, as Lambert, Hendricks, & Ross, multi-dubbed themselves to recreate an album's worth of classic Count Basie arrangements for the best selling long-player "Sing A Song Of Basie."

For a number of years, the big bands may have been the major attraction for dancers, but as Tommy Dorsey discovered when he still had the young Frank Sinatra under contract, for an incoming generation of young fans who gathered at the front of the stage, it was singers such as the scrawny Frankie (despite being publicly branded "the main reason for the rise in juvenile delinquency") who were now the prime focus of their dollar-waving attention. And it was these very same vocal stars who were to enjoy an unprecedented clear run when, on July 31, 1943, the American Federation of Musicians (AFM) instigated the first of two acrimonious nationwide recording bans, when only vocalists were able to make records.

At a time when swing had become king, musicians had become incensed with the use of their records by jukebox operators and radio stations without any royalty payments. When all efforts by the AFM to secure a fair deal for its members failed, a nationwide ban on all domestic recording was rigorously imposed.

In a totally unrelated incident that had taken place the previous year, the special services division of the US Armed Forces established a radio section producing top line variety shows such as *Command Performance*, *Jubilee*, and *G.I.Jive* for its new conscripts. Now, deprived of fresh material for its radio service, the top brass became so deeply concerned over the morale of its fighting men that it quickly began producing union-approved, exclusive-to-overseas-service personnel victory disks (V disks), which circumvented the ban.

Material was sourced from special recording sessions set up by V-disk producers, live concerts, radio broadcasts, movie soundtracks, a variety of established radio transcription services, and alternate/unissued takes of commercial recordings.

In the real world, those labels that hadn't stockpiled pre-ban recordings had to find a commercially acceptable compromise in double-quick time. If the ban heralded the cult of the crooner, it also confirmed its reliance on numerous vocal groups to supply a textured backdrop which, in turn, was a contributing factor to the pending demise of big band swing as a dominant force. Similarly, the use of jukeboxes, where formerly small combos had played, greatly reshaped the landscape for a generation determined to dump anything that suggested they were still tied to the family's apron strings.

But not every singer on the make followed the big band route. Innovative jazz stylists, from "club blues" pianist Nat King Cole to the original cool-cat trumpeter Chet Baker, emerged as popular singers somewhat by default, as did child actor Mel Tormé, who first attracted attention with his vocal group The Meltones. Elsewhere, pianist Nina Simone's ambitions were most definitely of a classical nature prior to her status as a politically motivated Diva.

Billy Eckstine, although by no means the first black crooner, was among the most commercially successful, crossing over to earn the tag "The Sepia Sinatra," score a succession of hit singles, and land a few cameos in Hollywood movies. For a period, both King Cole and Mr B were actually more popular with record fans than the self-proclaimed "Hoodlum from Hoboken." Frank, however, was never tagged "The Ofay Eckstine."

And then there was the formidable blues roar of such heavyweights as "The Boss of the Blues"—Kansas City shouter Joe Turner, the "Genius" that is Ray Charles, and the assertive presence of blues balladeers Joe Williams and Jimmy Witherspoon. These were artists who not only expanded the jazz vocabulary but, like Louis Jordan and Wynonie Harris before them, also laid cornerstones for the more imaginative aspects of emergent rock'n'roll: Turner nailing it down, in 1954, with "Shake, Rattle, and Roll" while, the following year, "Count Basie Swings/Joe Williams Sings" proved to be a *tour-de-force* album still without serious equal.

Before rock eventually took control of the charts in the mid 50s, the best-sellers were frequently influenced by cash-rich uptown US music publishers. It wasn't uncommon for half a dozen or more big name artists to record the same song and then vigorously compete against one another in the charts. As far as the fans were concerned, they could get a copy of a hot new tune recorded by the very object of their desire, which, in turn, was reflected by heavy chart action. In such an active climate, there were some singers who showed little restraint, until it seemed they were releasing a new single every two weeks.

Although it never degenerated into hand-to-hand combat, almost all available versions charted, the outsiders occasionally helped along by personal "charitable" donations to the influential dee-jays from eternally grateful song pluggers. The outcome was that almost everyone seemed to be a winner. However, most notably, it was the song publisher who, in some instances, scooped a larger royalty share than even the composer or the performer.

For instance, during one week in 1949, six entries on the US charts were devoted to recordings of "Some Enchanted Evening." Perry Como was No. 1, followed by Bing Crosby (3), Jo Stafford (4), Frank Sinatra (6), Ezio Pinza (7), and Paul Weston at No 9. This wasn't unique. The following year, eight versions of "Can Anyone Explain"—including individual versions from both Ella and Louis —filed into the Top 30 in the same week.

Whereas golden era vocalists had the big band circuit from which to launch themselves, today such outlets no longer exist. Those who choose such an arduous vocation have a much tougher task, and little chance to create the impact on vast audiences that this book's illustrious storytellers achieved. Yet despite the obstacles, there will always be those who will make a lasting impression, against the many who only allude to singing jazz, seduced by the myths and the allure of old photographs and album sleeves.

In reality, few past muster.

ROY CARR: EXECUTIVE EDITOR, IPC MUSIC PRESS

Left: California during the early 50s, and Billie Holiday performs one of the few twelve-bar blues songs in her repertoire, the self-penned "Fine And Mellow."

louis armstrong   17

records of the period before he was persuaded by his second wife, Lillian Hardin (who was also Oliver's pianist), to leave and join Fletcher Henderson's band in New York. Louis was with Henderson for a year, during which time he also recorded with a number of small groups, backing blues singers such as Bessie Smith, Ma Rainey, and Jimmie Rodgers.

However, it was with his own bands, the Hot Five and Hot Seven, that he found freedom to stretch out and establish a style that was distinct from the comparatively formularized New Orleans Dixieland format. Louis brought swing to jazz by loosening up the rigid ragtime rhythms and freeing the soloist (invariably himself, now on trumpet) from the restriction of the regular tempo.

Yet for many in his burgeoning audience, he was principally a singer and entertainer who spiced up the standard showstoppers of the day with a succession of perfectly pitched high notes and some effusive vocalizing. And it was this vocalizing that did for jazz singing what his trumpet did for instrumentalists, creating a template for the genre.

During the 1930s, Louis acquired a new manager, Joe Glaser, who was to stay with him throughout his career, and he found an even wider audience through a number of lucrative pop hits. Glaser also secured for Louis a succession of high-profile film parts, including *Pennies From Heaven* (1936) and *High Society* (1956), the latter with Bing Crosby and Frank Sinatra, which established Louis as an all-round family entertainer.

The advent of rock and roll in the 50s did little to diminish Louis' popularity, and he toured Europe with his six-piece outfit the All Stars to great acclaim as America's goodwill ambassador, with official sponsorship from the US State Department. Despite accusations that his repertoire had become routine and predictable, his fellow musicians unfailingly rallied to his defense, and for the remainder of his life Louis maintained his place as a much loved, avuncular figure for millions of music lovers around the world, many of whom would not otherwise have listened to jazz.

Louis Armstrong died in New York City on July 6, 1971, with, legend has it, a broad smile of satisfaction on his face.

The following interview was published by *Melody Maker* on December 24, 1955, at a time when Louis was re-recording his earlier classics with the All Stars for an audio autobiography. It comprised excerpts from another interview with Louis Armstrong in Paris, which was published in *US News and World Report*, December 2, 1955, under the title "They Cross The Iron Curtain To Hear American Jazz."

LOUIS & WAGNER AT THE MILAN OPERA HOUSE

We make no excuses for dwelling on the subject of Louis Armstrong. His European tour has reawakened interest in jazz in every country in which he has played. Now we give Louis' own impressions of the tour as reported by two editors of an American news magazine:-

Question: "Is there any difference between jazz as it's liked in Europe and jazz as it's liked in America?"

Louis: "It's the same all over the world. I always say a note's a note in any language if you hit it on the nose. But they appreciate the technical part of your music, every bit of it, everybody's been so classical-minded all over Europe. Back in Milan we was playing up at the Odeon, that's a concert hall two blocks from La Scala, the opera house, and after my concert I had to get in the cab and go over to La Scala and get pictures taken standing beside all these great men like Verdi and Wagner and their statues . . . right between 'em. That's what the Italians requested."

Question: "What kind of people do you get in your audience here...?"

Answer: "All kinds. Now the president of the Hot Club in Basle, Switzerland, is a old fellow, right old gentleman, and he's right on the ball.

"He's president of the Hot Club, and every one of them got all my jazz records—old fellow, he's a professor at the university."

Question: "Do you speak French at all, Louis?"

"A little bit, enough to get what I want. When I'd get to little towns I used to say, uh: 'Madame, Messieurs, maintenant we're gonna play "Them There Eyes."'—because they got the record, you don't need to say that in French.

"But I don't need to do that now: there's so many Frenchmen speakin' English."

LIKE WATER

"Pick up any Scandinavian?"

"'Skol,' I learned, yeah. When first got there it just looked like water to me and I got to be the skolinest cat you ever seen.

"And in Germany, what is it they say—'Prosit.' Yeah. Now them boys that slipped over the Iron Curtain to take in the concert—"

"You had some coming over from the Iron Curtain?"

"I didn't have them. They did it. In the Hot Club in Berlin these boys were there and one of them said, 'We slipped over the Iron Curtain to hear our Louis,' and they said 'We don't know how we gonna get back.'

"And I never heard of 'em since, but that's what they did."

Above: Preparing for a date in Stockholm, Sweden, in 1952.

Right: Louis visited Britain many times throughout his long career. Here, with trombonist Tyree Glenn, he makes an appearance on BBC television in 1965.

"They knew your music over there?"

"Sure, that's why they come—come over to hear me. If you don't believe it, lemme play in Russia and you'll have so many people goin' you'd think they was going to a football game. "

"So jazz is international?"

"Yeah, universal. All over the world. Japan—how many people would think the Japanese would dig our music the way they did?

"Why, all the trumpet players in Japan gave a dinner for me. Took my shoes off, you know, and sit down at this funny table and have a big meal—nothin' but the trumpets. . . ."

"Is it the same all over with jazz—no frontiers, no Iron Curtain?"

"That's right. Well, in Rome we was out at this beautiful home with them Italian diplomats an' all, and they're so proud.

"And I just happened to lift up my head and trumpet at the ceiling, and there was all the wonderful paintings you could think of—Mark Antony and Cleopatra and all them cats was up there, you know.

"Gee, they was lookin' right down at me. I don't know whether they was glad or sad but, man, we sure played."

PRESIDENT

"What is this Hot Club? Is there a Hot Club in every town in France?"

"Yes, sir; everywhere in Europe, most every town has a Hot Club. I'm honorary president of most of 'em."

Above: The All Stars during a concert tour of Britain in May 1956, with (l to r) Edmond Hall on clarinet, Louis, trombone man Trummy Young, and bass player Arvell Shaw.

"Are there Hot Clubs behind the Iron Curtain?

"There's got to be. Those are disciples. Those are my disciples. Guns or nothin' else couldn't keep them boys from comin' over to hear hot..

"Lots of them come from all over, but not all of them come up and speak. They don't want no trouble. They happened to be friends to Hans Blutner, this German boy, a big German cat; he brought them up to talk."

"Is it true that the president of France gave you a Sevres vase?"

"Oh, don't talk about that vase. When they come from the president with that vase I was upstairs with some cats talkin' and they come in and holler,'They is down there with that vase. Come on.' And down we go and they hand me this vase that cost a thousand dollars or somethin' like that—no, it was $5,000. Well, when I see this vase I say nobody gonna carry that for me—I'm gonna carry that myself.

"So I manage to get it to New York and I meet my wife Lucille there and the first thing I say is, 'Here you take this.' And it was wrapped in a towel and she thinks it's a bottle or somethin' and like to drop it. Well, she didn't and got it home in a special round black case, and you can see it there."

"In Europe you have crowds meeting you at railway stations and airports—does that happen in America?"

"No, not to that extent. Back home you're around and there's no wonder."

"How did things go when you played in Berlin?"

"Oh, fine, fine. There was these Berlin cats that wanted me to go and blow my trumpet at that there Russian soldier guardin' some Russian Red Army statue—you know, inside West Berlin—but I wouldn't.

"I could see this might be somethin' important to Russians and they might get the wrong idea. All I know is the horn, not politics or things like that."

JUST MUSIC

"Would a man like Molotov, the Soviet Foreign Minister, who's never heard any jazz, spark to it?

"Maybe. if he likes any good music."

"What do you play, Louis?"

"I just play music."

"Is it Dixie?"

"Any kind. I play music—you call it what you want."

"When everybody was swinging it, did you swing it too?"

"I swing right now. But I don't try to prove nothing—no more than just being a musician, that's all. You keep your tone—and that's what the younger generation is forgettin' about, tonation. . . ."

"Does it pay financially to come to Europe?"

"Well, we make out, but we don't think about money."

"Are you a religious man?"

"Yeah. I'm a Baptist and a good friend of the Pope's, and I always wear a Jewish star for luck."

THE "RIOTS"

"Have you ever met the Pope?"

"Yes. In 1949. Lucille had to wear a veil and everything. We stood there talkin'—he's a pleasant fellow. He said, 'I'm happy the people enjoy your music,'and he talk and I talk. "

"Tell us about that riot in Hamburg—what really happened there?"

"Nothing happened there. People just wanted us to play on some more. We played an encore. I took a bow with my shirt off but they still wouldn't go. The police tried to clear the hall for the next concert. But

they refused to go. Then the police turned the fire hose on them. The hall was a mess.

"The same thing happened in Roubaix, France. And in Lyons, too. They started throwin' things at the local band when they came back to take over. So the next night the owner put the brass band up in the balcony so they couldn't get hit. But the people didn't do anything to us."

"Are your audiences here more serious than they are in the US?"

"Yes, they are. They listen to jazz the way they listen to classical music. They make a study of it.

"In Turin, Italy, there was some little stinker in the audience, way up in the balcony. We were playin' 'Sleepy Time' and he made a little airplane out of a piece of paper and he must have been awfully good because it circled around and landed right on the stage. And about 15 Italians grabbed him.

"They grabbed him and said, 'One more time and we'll kill you.'"

"Is that because you're a famous artist?"

"No, it's because I'm playing something they want to hear."

"What about these American players over here, Louis? How would they do back home?"

"Mighty few would get along back in the States, mighty few. They get careless about their instruments, sloppy. Half of 'em don't practice."

HAPPINESS

"You play for the pleasure of it?"

"The pleasure and the people. It's happiness to me to see people happy."

"Well, what is jazz?"

"I wouldn't say I know what jazz is, because I don't look at it from that angle. We never did worry about what it was in New Orleans, we just always tried to play good. And the public named it. It was ragtime, Dixieland, gutbucket, jazz, swing, and it ain't nothin' but the same music."

"Where did you get 'Satchmo?'"

"'Satchmo' came from London. My name used to be 'Satchel Mouth'—you know, like a valise. Just a nickname. But when I got off the train the first time in London, Percy Brooks, who was the *Melody Maker* editor, say 'Hello, Satchmo.'

"I'll never forget Charlie Johnson, my trumpet player at the time. When he got there I say, 'Why did he call me Satchmo like that?' And he say, 'Because he thought you had more mouth.'"

"What do you think is the one thing you have that is the most important. That has made you a famous musician?"

"Well, determination and the love of my heart that nobody could persuade me to do otherwise."

"Louis, do you think hot jazz will end the Cold War?"

"If it's left to people that's peaceful with music, there wouldn't be no wars. Wouldn't be none. It comes from people that probably don't care so much about jazz."

ATOM JIVE

"Do you think the atomic bomb has made people go to music more than they did before?"

"Well, I don't dive into politics.

"Like in Geneva, that guy with the mike, you know. He would rush you with it. 'Well, what do you think of the Big Four Conference?' I say, "Well, I jus' hope that combo has a good time, and straightens out that jive."

Above: Satch mugs it for the camera in this still from the 1961 movie *Paris Blues*, with, in the background, the bass player Mort Herbert.

Above: Louis in his dressing room at a New York gig in the late 40s.

key recordings

1923	Louis' first recordings released as a member of King Oliver's band, including *"Chimes Blues."*
1924-5	Recordings with Fletcher Henderson Orchestra backing singers Bessie Smith (*"St Louis Blues"*), Ma Rainey (*"Counting the Blues"'*), and others.
1925	First of 33 sides recorded by Louis Armstrong and the Hot Five and Hot Seven include *"Cornet Chop Suey," "My Heart," "Hotter Than That,"* and *"Heebie Jeebies."*
1928	Release of *"West End Blues,"* one of 18 sides made with the Savoy Ballroom Five.
1929	*"Ain't Misbehavin"* from the revue *"Hot Chocolates"* introduces Louis to a wider public.
1929	*"Knockin' a Jug"* marked the first significant inter-racial jazz session featuring Jack Teagarden, Kaiser Marshall, and Eddie Lang.
1936	Hollywood film debut in *Pennies From Heaven.*
1947	*"Louis Armstrong Plays W.C.Handy"* LP tribute to "the Father of the Blues" with the All Stars. Arguably the best of "Pops" albums with the All Stars.
1947	Classic concert with Jack Teagarden captured for posterity on *"Louis Armstrong and the All Stars at Symphony Hall."* Sid Catlett's drum solo is an unexpected highlight.
1955	*"Satch Plays Fats"* features songs by Fats Waller.
1956	*"Satchmo: A Musical Autobiography"* reviews Louis' incomparable contribution to jazz in re-recordings.
1960	*"Bing and Satchmo"* LP. With specially written material by Johnny Mercer and sparkling arrangements by Billy May.
1961	*"Louis Armstrong and Duke Ellington: The Complete Collaborations."* A summit session from two living legends with the Duke sitting in on piano with the All Stars.
1964	*"Hello Dolly"* from the musical of the same name becomes a surprise world-wide multi-million-selling smash.
1970	*"Louis Armstrong and His Friends"* finds Louis in fine form on a diverse range of material by Lennon and McCartney and Pharoah Sanders.
1994	A surprise UK chart entry for the 20-year-old *"We Have All the Time in the World"* is swiftly followed by the compilation *"The Ultimate Collection."*

Chet Baker, graduate of the West Coast "cool" school, class of 1952, was born with the brooding good looks of a Hollywood film star and the musical talent to match. He was stealing scenes from his musical mentors from the age of 22 with a deceptively simple and beguiling trumpet technique, complemented by a languorous singing style in the Mel Tormé mold. The critics panned his singing for its obvious lack of finesse, and one label even edited out the vocal segments when reissuing his albums, but it was a sincere, open-hearted, and ingenuous sound, and as such had his female admirers in a swoon.

For a while in the mid-50s, Chet had it all, or so it seemed. Yet like the ill-fated hero of Dorothy Baker's sensationalist exposé of the jazz scene, *Young Man With A Horn*, Chet seemed destined to live his life acting out the role of the tortured genius of jazz, possessed by music and haunted by the specter of drug addiction.

He was born Chesney Henry Baker on December 23, 1929, in Yale, Oklahoma, moved to California in 1940, and there, at the age of 16, volunteered for the army, where he learned the rudiments of music and trumpet technique. In 1952, four years after his discharge from the service, Chet found himself a slot touring with the already legendary Charlie Parker, for whom he played the perfect foil, honing his refined, lyrical style against the master's intense flurry of notes until it shone with the luster of a legend in the making. Although Chet was only 22 when he left Bird later the same year to form his own outfit, Parker was sufficiently impressed to warn trumpet maestro Miles Davis, "You better watch out. There's a little white cat on the West Coast who is going to eat you up."

Chet's big break came when he joined the hot and hip Gerry Mulligan Quartet in 1952, staying long enough to take center stage as temporary leader when Mulligan was incarcerated on dope charges, before striking out with his own outfit. But Chet lacked leadership qualities, and some of his recordings reflect his lack of authority. Nevertheless, he was a consistent and popular poll winner throughout the 1950s, becoming something of an icon for teenager jazz aficionados and a role model for James Dean. Chet had stayed clean of hard drugs until his friend and pianist Richard Twardzick died suddenly from a heroin overdose in 1955 while on tour with the Baker quartet. Twardzick's death sent Chet into a spiral of depression, in which he was easy bait for the predatory attentions of the pushers who fed off him from that time until his death.

Although drugs ravaged his looks and wrecked his private life, they rarely soured the sweet tone of his music. Both as an instrumentalist and singer, Chet characterized the mellow, introspective, cool school of jazz that held sway on the West Coast during the mid-50s, in contrast to the hard bop fraternity wailing loud and proud in New York.

Chet's increasing dependence on hard drugs coincided with the decline of cool jazz, and at the end of the decade he found himself in jail on Riker's Island, stripped of his cabaret card, which had enabled him to play the New York club circuit. Without his meal ticket he was forced to work abroad for much of the 60s, recording for anyone and everyone who pushed a contract under his nose and a pen into his hand. But he was often busted and deported for alleged narcotics offenses while the ink was still drying. During that time, and against all the odds and expectations, he managed to make a series of superb LPs for Prestige, including "Groovin," "Cool Burnin," and "Smokin," on which he played flugelhorn exclusively. Singing to impress the ladies was no longer a priority; by then, playing to eat and stay faithful to his muse was all that mattered.

Back in San Francisco in 1968, he hit the skids so hard that it looked as if he might be out for the count. A welcoming committee of dope-dealing thugs beat him so badly that he had to have his remaining teeth pulled out and replaced by dentures. Down and disillusioned, he pawned his horn, turned his back on music, and lived on welfare handouts for much of the 70s.

Incredibly, when he eventually returned to music he was still able to shine on stage when the mood took him—for example, recording a stunningly good set in Tokyo just a year before his death. But for a man who was the jazz icon of his generation, the end was as tragic as anything in Dorothy Baker's novel. Chet Baker fell to his death from a second-story hotel window in Amsterdam on May 13, 1988. It remains a mystery as to whether it was an accident or murder.

The interview with Mike Nevard took place in June 1953 while Chet was completing his apprenticeship with the Gerry Mulligan Quartet. A few months later, the quartet found itself leaderless when Mulligan became a guest of the US Government, leaving Chet to take over.

MULLIGAN'S ON A "WORSHIP" KICK
SAYS HIS MULTI WONDER-MAN CHET BAKER

Chet Baker looks like a boy, plays like a genius, and talks like a man. The most sensational trumpet discovery since Diz and Miles has some pungent things to say about Gerry Mulligan, big-headedness, lectures, and jazz.

You read all about Chet Baker's trumpet work last week. Steve Race described his ideas as "fluent, always thoughtful;" Dill Jones referred to him as "one of the greatest white players ever."

Chet Baker's work with the Gerry Mulligan Quartet puts him in the super class. As we said last week, the personal integration of Mulligan and Baker is incredible. Instrumentally, he is as important to the Gerry Mulligan Quartet as Gerry Mulligan himself.

"BIG-HEADED GERRY"

As soon as our dissection of the Quartet was under way, and the analysts were laying the pieces on the table, we cabled Howard Lucraft in Hollywood for up-to-the-minute data on Baker.

First thing to come to light is that Chet has just waxed his own Quartet LP for Pacific. Second thing is that Chet Baker has some pretty

Previous page: The first publicity photo session with the Chet Baker Quartet by William Claxton, 1954.

Right: Chet with pianist Russ Freeman, recording "The Thrill Is Gone" for the *Chet Baker Sings* album. Another shot by William Claxton.

Below: William Claxton captured Chet on stage at the Forum Theatre in Los Angeles in 1957, recording the LP *Chet Baker and Crew*.

Left: From another of
the landmark 1954
vocal sessions, Chet at
the microphone shot
by William Claxton, one
of the world's greatest
jazz photographers.

Opposite: A famous
Claxton image, Chet at
the piano during the
same sessions. The
photographer calls this
"Young Beethoven."

straightforward views on jazz and jazzmen. "Gerry Mulligan is a great musician," he says. "But too many people have been telling him he's a genius; especially his previous wife. Gerry now walks around thinking he is the greatest thing that ever happened to jazz. I've told Gerry what I think of his attitude."

That's mighty powerful talk coming from a musician who's only arrived on the jazz scene in that last year or so. In 1942, Chet Baker wasn't even a musician. He was a non-player in junior high school. However, that was the year he started to learn. He had lessons at the school's instrumental training class. They were the only lessons he ever had. "I'm really self-taught," he says. "I play very unorthodox; finger Bb open, etc."

On November 5, 1946, at the age of 16, Chet quit school and joined the army.

"I said I was 17 and got in. They sent me to Germany. I was a 'typist.' But in 1947, while in Berlin, I got in an army band."

LEARNED BY EAR

Chet still wasn't a reading musician. He learned marches by ear, and picked up reading by playing the marches he had learned and comparing the notes played with those on paper.

His main musical interest then was symphony concerts. But late in 1947 he heard jazz; Stan Kenton came into his life via V-disks.

"When I heard those I didn't really know what was happening. I heard the 'Artistry' things, 'Intermission Riff,' etc. As a newcomer to jazz, I found them inspiring."

What does he think now?

"Jazz will evolve into a fusion of jazz and contemporary classical music, I think. No, not like Stan Kenton—more with small groups.

"I look forward to Gerry, myself, Stan Getz, and Bob Brookmeyer in a pianoless group. Bob is a fantastic valve trombonist currently with Getz.

"There would have to be more ensemble—not so much of a solo sound. Everyone would play a line —extemporized, of course.

"Dixieland? Well, Dixieland is so limited melodically and they always have that bass thing going with the left hand of the piano and trombone, etc."

Yet despite Baker's references to Dixieland, and the perfect co-ordination of his playing with Mulligan, this young trumpeter is no stickler for the rules.

In 1948, after being demobbed, he went to El Camino College in Lawndale. California, to study theory, harmony, etc. He failed his course.

"I don't know if I failed because it was so easy, or because I just couldn't see it. At college they did nothing but study rules and then throw them out.

"I wanted to do things by ear. To me, if it sounds right it is right.

"Maybe this rule stuff is all right for those who have no ear or creative ability."

It was while taking his course that Chet started playing jazz. He sat in at college dances and took on a few casual dates. Then, in 1949, he broke into a few of the Hollywood jazz cliques—in particular, the Monday night jam session at the North Hollywood Showtime Club, where the tenor player Dave Pell and other members of the Les Brown band got together.

"At first they just let me play one chorus at the end of the evening. Then every succeeding Monday I got to play a little more, until finally I got the job there."

"I CREATE"

Then, in 1951, Chet did a surprising thing. He re-enlisted in the army— and went straight into an army band in San Francisco.

"That's when I really got to make it in jazz," he says. For, in San Francisco, Chet sat-in nearly every night at Bop City, playing with Dexter Gordon, Teddy Edwards, Hampton Haws, Cal Tjader, Paul Desmond, Nick Exposito, etc.

Did the playing there influence Chet? "Frankly, I've never listened too much or copied anybody.

"I never had a record player until a year ago. I try not to remember the things I play. I create from the start each time.

"With the Quartet, we play the same tunes to the same audience all the time. But Gerry said once that my approach to music was completely different to any other musician—more fresh and original."

WITH PARKER

It was too original for Chet to get stuck with an army band anyway, and in April 1952 he was out again playing towns up and down the Pacific coast with Vido Musso.

A month later, Charlie Parker heard him and fixed him for his group at the Hollywood Tiffany Club.

"Naturally I liked the opportunity to work with Parker. Of course, he hasn't changed at all in his playing really for ten years. Also, he is on this 'worship' kick like Gerry Mulligan. This must affect a guy's playing."

It was soon after this, incidentally, that Chet Baker and Gerry Mulligan met. Chet had been with the Art Pepper group at The Cottage in San Pedro, and met Gerry at a jam session in the valley. The "valley'" is North Hollywood.

GERRY'S LECTURES

"Gerry seemed to like the way I played. He asked me to do a record session with him for Prestige. I didn't make the session eventually, as I had an argument with Gerry's then wife. As it turned out the records weren't very good."

Then Gerry went into the Haig with his pianoless quartet. Chet went with him and has been with the group ever since.

Recently, in American papers, there have been stories of Mulligan addressing vindictive lectures to his audiences. What did his trumpeter think of these?

"Maybe it's all right for Gerry to give the customers lectures about keeping quiet while he's playing. But when these lectures last 15 minutes or more it gets a little embarrassing for the rest of us on the stand— to say the least.

"Gerry shouldn't keep knocking other musicians, either."

Baker's remarks about his baritone-playing boss are certainly revealing. And they reveal not only Mulligan's personal character, but also the self-assuredness of the man who made them.

They fit neatly with Baker's remarks that "eventually I want to have my own band." And he is, in fact, already recording with his own unit.

How much longer will the fascinating patterns woven by Mulligan and Baker flow from wax? How much longer will we hear the intelligent sounds of the group that has had so much influence on contemporary jazz thinking?

"Why, even Stan Getz is changing," says Chet Baker. "He is not trying to be so polished. He's more relaxed, blowing more, swinging more. I think our quartet made him change that way.

"He doesn't seem to be so afraid of making mistakes. In our quartet we might make a hundred mistakes a night, but we're trying to create all the time."

Yes, Chet Baker talks like a man.

Let's hope he thinks like one. The Gerry Mulligan Quartet without Mulligan, or without Baker, would be a tragedy.

30

Left: Young man with a horn. In the studio at the height of his fame as a jazz icon in 1954.

Above: Baker brought the misty style of his trumpet playing to his work as a jazz vocalist—here in session with tenor sax player Jack Montrose and alto sax man Herb Geller. Photo by William Claxton.

key recordings

1952	First recordings with the Gerry Mulligan Quartet
1953	LPs *"West Coast Live"* featuring Stan Getz and *"Witchdoctor"* with the Lighthouse All-stars.
1954	*"Chet Baker Sings"* 10" LP on Pacific Jazz. The label reissued the album two years later with extra tracks to make a 12" LP and again in the 1960s overdubbed with guitar by Joe Pass to simulate stereo! Currently available as *"The Best of Chet Baker Sings."*
1956	*"Playboys"* with Art Pepper.
1958	*"Chet Baker in New York"*—a summit meeting of the *"cool"* and *"hard bop"* brigade.
1959	*"Chet"* LP classic ballad showcase featuring Bill Evans and Pepper Adams.
1962	*"The Italian Sessions"* recorded during a five-year European exile during which he recorded numerous albums of varying quality.
1965	Released *"Groovin," "Coming On," "Cool Burnin," "Smokin,"and "Boppin" with the Chet Baker Quintet"* later reissued as *"Lonely Star." "Stairway to the Stars"* and *"On a Misty Night."*
1974	*"Chet Baker and Lee Konitz in Concert."*
1974-7	*"Chet Baker and Paul Desmond Together—The Complete Studio Recordings"* Chet dueling with Dave Brubeck's horn hero and coming off the clear winner.
1979	*"Daybreak"* and *"The Touch of Your Lips"* on both of which Chet is backed just by guitar (Doug Raney) and bass (N H Orsted Pedersen).
1984	*"Blues For A Reason"* with Warne Marsh on tenor sax.
1986	*"Chet Baker Featuring Van Morrison Live at Ronnie Scot's."*
1987	*"In Tokyo"* 2CD Live set.
1995	*"The Legacy"* posthumous release of an exceptionally fine concert performance from 1987 recorded in Hamburg with a national radio big band.

Sinatra afforded Tony Bennett the ultimate accolade when he called him "the best singer in the business," although Bennett tends to play down his success by making light of the plaudits generously heaped on him. "I was the Madonna of my day," he once remarked. "I just didn't take my clothes off."

The singer who many now identify with his biggest hit, "I Left My Heart in San Francisco," made his name with a string of jazz-influenced pop ballads in the 1950s, but his first love has always been jazz and his finest recordings showcase his innate sense of swing and a cultured sophistication. While it is undeniable that he owes his wide and enduring popularity to the string of smooth Las Vegas-styled showstoppers that he recorded in the 1960s, his collaborations with some of the greatest names in jazz have earned him the unqualified admiration of his peers and the respect of the critics.

In a career spanning five decades, he has worked with some of the undisputed giants of jazz, including Count Basie, Bill Evans, Stan Getz, Gene Krupa, Herbie Mann, Dexter Gordon, Joe Marsala, George Benson, and Dizzy Gillespie, all of whom would willingly endorse Bennett's election to the jazz Hall of Fame.

Tony Bennett was born Antonio Dominick Benedetto on August 3, 1926, in Queens, New York. The son of a grocer, Bennett believed that success would only come through tenacity and hard graft, and so he worked his way up the hard way, taking jobs as a singing waiter during his teens and doing the round of TV talent shows under the name Joe Bari.

It was through an appearance on the Arthur Godfrey show in 1950 that he came to the attention of Pearl Bailey and Bob Hope, who helped to secure him a recording contract with Columbia. However, he was burdened with second-rate material by producer Mitch Miller, and for the first crucial year he failed to score a hit.

He finally got his break the following year after persuading the label's house arranger, Percy Faith, to let him record "Because Of You" while Miller was on vacation. Faith's tasteful arrangement, rich in counter melodies and mellow woodwinds, was the ideal setting for the singer's urbane, bel canto style, and helped propel the single to the number one spot.

A second number one that same year was an unlikely but compelling cover version of Hank Williams' country classic "Cold Cold Heart," to be followed by a unbroken stream of hits in the American charts over the following 16 years, including 24 that made the Top 40.

From 1962, parallel to his "pop" success, Bennett began to establish himself as an album artist, chalking up 25 hit LPs in the ten years to 1972. During the same period, he increased his standing with the cognoscenti by making selective appearances on the concert platform—including a celebrated set at Carnegie Hall in 1962—and by recording a series of prestigious jazz albums in illustrious company. These included solo sets with pianist Bill Evans in the late 70s, a duet with Ray Charles, and a number of tasteful tributes to the classic American songwriters and singers, including Fred Astaire and Bennett's old buddy Frank Sinatra.

Bennett's staunchly held Roman Catholic convictions made him wary of show business and of the compromises that he feared he would be forced to make. For this reason, his concert and television appearances were always highly selective, preventing him from building sufficient momentum to offer a serious challenge to Sinatra, and giving the impression that he was capricious and inconsistent.

For much of the 1980s, Bennett appeared to turn his back on show business, indulging instead in his passion for painting and attending major exhibitions of his work in Paris, New York, San Francisco, Los Angeles, and London, all of which were held under his real name. But the hiatus came to an unexpected end in 1993 when the stylish promo video for the single "Stepping Out" was playlisted on MTV, and the 67-year-old singer found himself lauded as the epitome of cool sophistication. The offer of an Unplugged session followed, to which he laconically replied, "I've always been unplugged."

On the back of his new, fashionable image, he was coaxed to perform with the Lemonheads and the Red Hot Chilli Peppers, asked to appear at Woodstock II, and was persuaded to appear in a Nike commercial. But the biggest surprise and an indisputable highlight of his career was still to come—the winning of a Grammy Award for Album of the Year in 1994.

This interview, published in *Melody Maker* on October 23, 1965, was conducted by Leonard Feather in Hollywood.

TONY BENNETT: A GAS TO SING WITH BIG BANDS

Jazz, which could use a few foul-weather friends these days, has no more staunch partisan than Tony Bennett.

Whether Bennett is a jazz singer is one of those moot questions, like "Why is there air?" and will be left unanswered here.

The closeness and effectiveness of his relationship with jazz, however, is beyond quibble.

Bennett, currently busy with his first straight, dramatic, non-singing movie role (in *The Oscar*), is getting his kicks on weekends singing at Hollywood's Playboy Club with the trio of Ralph Sharon, who before joining the singer as musical director 14 years ago, was the winner of several *Melody Maker* polls as Britain's No. 1 jazz pianist.

EXPOSED

"I started doing concerts with Count Basie's band back around 1958," says Bennett. "It was almost that long ago, too, that I played the Americana Hotel in Florida with Duke Ellington's band. I can't tell you what dates like these meant in terms of musical education. It was a priceless experience for me and my musicians.

"Before that time, I had stuck to café jobs mostly with local house bands plus Ralph's rhythm section. But with these bands I got into an entirely different state of mind—working with Count is different from working with Duke, because one band roars and the other band growls.

Above: Like all the great song stylists that came out of the big band era, Tony Bennett surrounded himself with the very best musicians for recording sessions and live dates.

"Woody Herman's band and its spirit always were perfect for me, too. This fall, after a couple of Nevada dates, I'm going to go on tour with Woody.

"The reason I play with these people is twofold. First, as I say, it's musically stimulating; but also, I notice there are so many pessimists in the business today who say nothing is happening. Well, it's easy to disprove that.

"Ella Fitzgerald put together a show in Los Angeles a few months ago with me and Basie's band and the Oscar Peterson Trio. It was on a Monday night, the worst evening of the week; and the very same night there was a big show at another concert hall in town, with Stan Kenton's Neophonic Orchestra. So we broke all the rules, yet the house was packed, and everybody walked out looking as if they'd enjoyed themselves thoroughly.

"I think the entertainers should combine and play together a lot more. Jack Jones or Nancy Wilson with Woody Herman would make an exciting package for every college in the country. The singers with the big bands as a team make a better balance; it reminds you of the days when Sinatra worked with Tommy Dorsey."

ROARS

Bennett has an unusual theory about the excitement provided by today's orchestras. "Duke and Woody and the Count travel all over the US and visit every country on earth. They end up with something so much more on the ball musically, being exposed to all the peoples and cultures of the world.

"The average studio musician that stays home with the wife and the swimming pool can't broaden his horizons. But a musician who has been to Pakistan, to Russia, to Brazil, is stimulated into a more varied and exciting performance."

Bennett is a staunch defender of the jazz avant garde, and draws the analogy with painting. "Paul Klee once said that if the world were sane, everybody would want a painting of a tree to look just like a tree. But modern art goes so many different ways.

"It's a matter of taste and careful listening. If you like an Ornette Coleman, fine; if not, that's understandable, but you can't deny the artistry and effort that went into it."

Maybe the time has come for singers to bring the combos back, too. During Bennett's comments about the new jazz, a wild picture flashed through my mind: Tony on tour with accompaniment by the Ornette Coleman Quartet. Memo to George (Newport) Wein and Jimmy (Monterey) Lyons: Are you ready for this?

Subtitled "Tony Bennett on looking for a hit" the interview below by Alan Walsh appeared on November 20, 1965.

WHY I DIDN'T WANT TO DO "YESTERDAY"

Tony Bennett is revered by most lovers of "class" music. But even Bennett, the man whose "San Francisco" has become a standard, has been sniped at by critics all over the world. They have maintained that the Bennett voice sounds flat on occasion.

"I think that in the early days they were possibly right, that my pitching was slightly off on occasion," Tony told me in his suite at London's Hilton Hotel. "But that was in the early days. Not now. Now I know I don't sing flat.

"As long as the piano and the band is in tune, I know I am too, and we have a ball."

Left: Bennett, always the consummate perfectionist, analyzes an arrangement.

Below: In the studio— Hollywood in the mid 1960s.

**Above: Tony Bennett
in a recording session
during a visit to Britain,
photographed by David
Redfern.**

Tony, here for the Royal Variety Show, regarded the honor of meeting the Queen so highly that he stayed on over the weekend to watch the tape of the show on TV on Sunday.

"The show was one of my highspots, it had magic for me. This whole trip has provided me with many memorable moments.

"Sharing a dressing room with Jack Benny, for instance. In the United States, he's an Old Master of show business and it was just a great thing to be working with him here. I'll take many memories back to America with me."

PHENOMENON

"I like the musical appreciation in Britain. For example, the Beatles. I admire the way that they have hit so big. There's a lot of room to sit down and analyze the phenomenon. I like the fact that four young men have got so far.

"I think they are imaginative and they will end up as top artists in whatever sphere they might progress to, although their music is not exactly my bag.

"Many people have said to me: 'You should record "Yesterday,"' but when I sat down and thought about it, there were already 25 versions out. I liked the song very much and I would have liked to have had the first 'class' recording of it. I don't like that word 'class' too much. I'm a pop singer, I sing popular songs.

"There are some very good teenage records about. But I don't like the sense of juvenile delinquency which is reflected in the tonality of some records. I like teenage music if it's got a good dance beat, and decent lyrics. I don't like teenage music that lacks taste.

"I think that it's a good thing that these young performers can work before the public. When I was young, I was in a group which tried all over Broadway for work."

INTEGRITY

"People said we were very good but inexperienced. It took us seven years to get onto a stage. I think it's good that there is the opportunity for these young artists to appear.

"I'm still concerned with making hit records, but records that I feel mean something and have musical integrity. I could make a hit tomorrow by just singing something with a hillbilly beat. But I wouldn't feel it. I have to believe in a song before I can release it.

"I took a whole summer deciding how and whether to record one number. I'm glad I did because it turned out very well. That was 'The Shadow Of Your Smile.'

"Do I still enjoy singing 'San Francisco?' Yes, I still feel that song as much now as when I first did it four years ago. It was a wonderful song and I still get that emotional thrill from it.

"I'd like to see the fine songwriters around today getting more recognition—people like Cy Coleman, Joe McCarthy Jr, and Lalo Schifrin. They are an extension of the Jerome Kerns and Cole Porters and don't get enough recognition. They are forced wrongly to take a back seat.

"I also enjoy working with jazz musicians. I was very impressed with the musicians I've heard in Britain. In particular, I enjoyed the saxophone player at Annie's Room, Pete King.

"Jazz musicians play with spontaneity and emotion. You never have to ask them to play with more feeling. Because that's what they are most concerned with."

Left: Tony in action, April 1965.

Above: On tour in the UK, shot by London-based Dezo Hoffman.

Above: Tony has kept crooning through the 80s and 90s in his gray-haired years.

key recordings

1950 Secured Columbia contract through Bob Hope and Pearl Bailey recommendation plus strength of early demos including *"Boulevard of Broken Dreams."*

1951 First hit *"Because of You"/"I Won't Cry Anymore"* (No. 1 in US, 31 weeks on the chart). Follow up *"Cold Cold Heart"* also No. 1 same year.

1953 Third No.1 *"Rags to Riches," "Stranger in Paradise,"* (No. 3) from hit musical ***Kismet*** based on a melody by classical composer Alexander Borodin.

1956 *"Just In Time"* from the musical ***Bells Are Ringing*** becomes the first standard to be specifically associated with Bennett.

1958 *"In Person"* LP with Count Basie

1962 Multi-million-selling single *"I Left My Heart in San Francisco"* and album of the same name arranged by Robert Farnon.

1962 *"At Carnegie Hall"* double LP.

1972 *"The Good Things in Life"* LP last to chart until the 1990s.

1973 *"Sings the Rodgers and Hart Songbook"* LP with the Ruby Braff-Georges Barnes Quartet.

1977 *"Beautiful Music"* (aka *"Make Magnificent Music"*) live LP with Marian and Jimmy McPartland.

1978 *"Together Again"* album with pianist Bill Evans.

1986 *"The Art of Excellence"* co-produced by his son Danny and featuring a trio led by Bennett's long-time musicial director Ralph Sharon. Album featured duet with Ray Charles.

1987 Double disk anthology *"Tony Bennett/Jazz"* including previously unreleased material.

1987 *"Bennett and Berlin"* LP featuring guests Dizzy Gillespie, George Benson, and Dexter Gordon.

1992 *"Perfectly Frank"* tribute LP to Sinatra.

1994 Grammy Award for the album *"Unplugged."*

1995 *"Here's to the Ladies"* tribute LP to female singers such as Doris Day and Billie Holiday.

1995 Four-CD box set *"Forty Years: The Artistry of Tony Bennett."*

It was Ray Charles who once famously attempted to define the elusive quality of jazz by naming one of his LPs "Genius Plus Soul Equals Jazz." It is as good a description of the music as one is likely to get, although both the form and Ray himself defy definition.

Many musicologists and more than a few of the man's fans might classify Ray as a soul singer, and yet he doesn't get a mention on Arthur Conley's classic song "Sweet Soul Music," on which Conley name-checks the great soul singers of the 60s as if he is reciting a roll of honor.

Ray didn't make the roll, not because he doesn't rate as a soul singer, but because he strides like a colossus across several categories, casting his awesome shadow on gospel, R&B, southern white country, and even Tin Pan Alley, before staking his claim to be a jazz singer with soul.

In a career spanning over 50 years, Ray has steadfastly refused to limit himself to one specific style. His restless eclecticism and eagerness to please has occasionally led to compromise, although fortunately not on his jazz albums, where his voice soars with the aspiration of a gospel minister, testifying with the intensity and conviction of one who has sinned and then returned to the fold.

Born Ray Charles Robinson on September 23, 1932, in Albany, Georgia, he was cast in the mold of the tragic jazz hero—blinded at six from the eye disease glaucoma and orphaned at 15. Yet he has had the last laugh at Fate.

He would later remark with uncharacteristic bitterness that he was destined to succeed because he had everything going against him—he was black, born in the South, and blind from an early age—factors that made him ferociously determined to make his mark. By his teens he had taught himself to play alto sax and piano using Braille. As soon as he had mastered his instruments, he discovered an innate ability for composing, although he didn't record his own tunes until he felt that he was sufficiently established.

His initial influence was Nat King Cole, whose songs supplied much of the repertoire for his first professional trio, which began playing dates in 1947. But a liking for the blues and gospel gave his music and his voice an edge that initially caught the ear of a TV producer in the Pacific Northwest. Securing a regional TV slot gave Ray a substantial, ready-made audience to whom he pitched the first of a series of R&B sides using Lowell Fulson's hard-driving blues band, all of which went on to become hits when released by Swingtime between 1949 and 1952.

A year later, Ray made the move to Atlantic, and there, stimulated by success, he felt sufficiently confident to record a clutch of self-penned songs bolstered by a few gospel standards to which he had added his own lyrics.

His first album, "The Great Ray Charles," was a straight jazz set with all the trimmings: strings, backing vocalists, and support from seasoned sidemen from the Duke Ellington and Count Basie bands. By the time the more commercial follow-up, "The Genius of Ray Charles," was released in 1959, Ray had already earned the title the Genius, and scored his first multi-million-selling single with the seminal gospel-styled call-and-response opus "What'd I Say," which launched "soul" as a by-product of rhythm and blues to a worldwide audience.

His subsequent hits (32 between 1957 and 71) alternated between blues-tinged pop and country-style ballads, although even on his most schmaltzy offerings he seldom sold a song short. There was no trace of crowd-pleasing compromise on the bona fide jazz albums with which he kept his credibility during the 50s, 60s, and 70s; indeed, Ray Charles has been cited as a seminal influence on jazz giants such as Horace Silver and Charles Mingus, and the beat writers Allen Ginsberg and Jack Kerouac.

In the final analysis, Ray's restless eclecticism may have undermined his achievements, but his influence on jazz and popular music is inestimable. Comedian Bill Cosby gave some indication of his significance in a classic routine in which he described Columbus sailing to America in the hope of discovering Ray Charles.

Prior to a British tour that commenced on September 26, 1969, Ray Charles was featured in a two-page spread interview by *Melody Maker*'s man in Hollywood, Leonard Feather.

A FIGHTER WHO HAS WON THE TOUGHEST BATTLES

The business tycoon swiveled in his office chair and fingered a Braille edition of *Dr Tom Dooley: My Story*. The scene was a business building owned by him on Washington Boulevard in Los Angeles, its second floor taken up by his recording studio and numerous other ventures (RPM Enterprises), the rest profitably rented out. As I was shown into his handsome, conservatively decorated office, he picked up a phone to talk briefly with Joe Adams, his suave ex-actor major domo, then leaned back in the chair. For the next hour or two Ray Charles, now 37, graying a little around the temples, and at relative peace with the world, rapped about life, race, and the career that has brought him, among other comforts, an annual income well into the seven-figure bracket and a couple of private planes, one a jet.

Having recently read the galley proofs of a book due out soon—*The Sound of Soul* by a sensitive black writer named Phyl Garland—I wondered what would be his reaction to Miss Garland's assessment of the early Charles as "a young man in his 20s . . . whose voice sounded indescribably old."

"Many people have said that," said Charles. "Hearing me on records, they'd picture me as a huge, aging fellow, about six feet six and 250 pounds. That's the sound they hear."

PRECISE

"Soul? I don't have a precise definition, but there were certain real old blues singers—Big Boy Crudrup, Tampa Red, Washboard Sam, Muddy

Above: Ray in a still from the 1964 feature film *Ballad In Blue*, which was made in Ireland and released in America with the title *Blues For Lovers*.

Above: An animated Ray in front of a 70s line-up, shot in Paris.

Above Right: In the recording studio on July 4, 1962.

Left: The full Charles experience featuring the 16-piece orchestra (plus Ray) and the 4-piece vocal group The Raelettes.

Waters, Blind Boy Phillips—I was raised with their sounds, so this certainly was a part of me, and it was the same as being reared in a Baptist church.

"Nat Cole—I tried like the devil to sing like him, but his influence had nothing to do with the blues or soul sound. What mainly attracted and influenced me was his piano playing."

Miss Garland also makes the point that middle-class Negroes, previously ashamed of their heritage, now say it loud: they are black and they are proud.

"There is some little truth in that, to the extent that certain people are brainwashed by white society. When I was a youngster, what we now call soul music was known as race music, and you didn't hear it on the radio.

"Some black people felt they were on the bottom of the pile anyhow, and since blues singers were looked down upon—this was as low as you could get in the music field—by associating with it, they would identify with the bottom of that bottom. But that's not a general rule —there are plenty of colored people who have followed my career for years and years and who certainly wouldn't qualify for the poverty program."

The man who grew to adolescence under the unspeakable triple burden of blackness, blindness, and poverty, speaks now in the temperate terms of a middle-class moderate. His reactions often are those of a black capitalist and realist, a ghetto graduate who may actually believe in the American dream because through most of his adult life, it has been a part of his experience. ("I Got A Woman," his first real hit, was recorded in 1954 when he was 22.)

Still, the shell of success could not have rendered him invulnerable to the slings and needles of outrageous racism. It was not until 1965 that he entered a Los Angeles hospital to post a milestone on the road to maturity by curing himself permanently of the narcotics addiction that had been a heritage of teenage ghetto life.

The raging turmoil of the pre-cure Charles soon gave way to a calmer personality. After all the years of naked anguish he seemed to have come to terms with himself and with society.

He is as far from Uncle Tommery as from militancy. When the subject of protest songs came up, he said, "It's sort of fashionable now. I will not do a song just because it's the in thing to do." But he quickly added that he had recorded, a few years ago, two tunes that might be classified in the protest category. (But what, some militants may say, has he protested for us lately?)

CHOICE

His present conservatism in the choice of material carries over into his attitude toward freakout electronic sounds. "I played electric piano long before it was popular—remember 'What'd I Say' in 1959?—but not all these things sound good to me. The sax has a nice sound when the amplifier is set right, but you saw my show at the Coconut Grove— nobody in my band plays one. I haven't tried electric sax myself. I don't need to, because I can hear in my mind's ear precisely just how it would sound, just as I could write a whole big band arrangement right at this desk without ever going over to the piano.

"The Moog synthesizer is interesting—I'd like to give that a whirl some day."

Turning to the related topic of the rock volume syndrome, and the deaf generation predicted for us by Ralph Nader and by prominent ear specialists, he said: "That's been proven for many years; I don't need any doctor to tell me that you can take any piercing sound and drive someone deaf. I can even take a medium frequency, say 1000 cycles, and drive you deaf. That's why I know the kids can't possibly stick with it. Five years from now there'll be some other fad."

The generation gap means this to him: "In my young days, if you went from, say, Tampa to Chicago, you came back and told everybody in town about it; today, by the time a kid is 15, he may have been to Europe and back. They're not necessarily more sophisticated, just more experienced, and they're exposed to more than they can absorb and handle. It's like, you can overwork a computer; if you put too much in, it'll holler."

SOCIETY

"Our kids are right in many ways—90 percent of them are righter than we are—but our society has put so much pressure on them, with so many gigantic problems and dangers, that they try to escape through forms of behavior that we don't understand. To put things right, we adults are going to go through a lot of changes in our own ideas and attitudes."

It was when we discussed the business end of music that Ray Charles, the soul singer, was instantly transformed into the president of RPM Enterprises. I confronted him with the materialistic credo as voiced recently by a major record company executive: "If any artist can't sell 100,000 records, we are not interested in that artist."

"I don't find that so callous," said Charles. "It's the way things have to be. With the production costs as they are nowadays, most artists can't break even unless they can sell 50,000 to 100,000. Even back in the 1950s, Atlantic didn't hire me to experiment with; they hired me to make money, and they had a good idea of what my potential was.

"In any case, the very big record companies do make exceptions. Look at all the classical music that is recorded. Almost none of the classics get anywhere near the sales of a country and western hit, but at RCA or Columbia they can afford to round out their catalogs by including them."

Charles is no less pragmatic in his personal appearances. "A guy who comes in to hear my R&B songs will sit still for a ballad and maybe learn to appreciate this other kind of music, or vice versa. I check the reactions of people. Generally, my guide lines are how the records go. By the same token, a tune that hit first in the black community will be established later with whites, just as 'Georgia' and 'Crying Time' hit with whites and later with blacks. In the final analysis all audiences are pretty much alike.

"In New York we played exactly the same show at the Copa as at the Apollo Theater."

REASONS

"One of the key reasons I'm still around is that we try to have a show that's as well rounded as possible, with something for the fan whether his bag be soul, country and western, modern jazz, or what have you."

Ray Charles, multi-millionaire, knows the fine print in every contract he signs, knows better than some of his own engineers how to run his own recording equipment and his airplanes. As a fighter who has won some of the toughest battles of our society, he has emerged a whole man, his mind crammed with knowledge of a host of subjects from sociology to psychiatry.

A studio shot of Ray Charles in the crucial period in the late 50s when he was blending blues and gospel as one of the founding pioneers of what would become soul music. Here, in a picture by William Claxton, Charles is with one of his backing vocal group the Raelettes.

4 6

key recordings

1949 Ray's first recordings are made with his first trio in Seattle.

1953 After a propitious move to Atlantic Ray finds his style with *"It Should've Been Me," "Losing Hand."* and *"Mess Around."*

1954 Releases of the first of his self-penned songs become hits, *"Hallelujah I Love Her So," "Come Back Baby," "Don't You Know,"* and *"I Got A Woman"* (covered by Elvis Presley).

1954 Ray backs Guitar Slim on *"The Things I Used to Do,"* a No. 1 hit in the R&B chart.

1957 Debut LP *"The Great Ray Charles"* was in essence a jazz album with soulful backing from a female quartet, The Raelettes.

1957 *"Swanee River Rock"* becomes Ray's first Top 40 hit.

1957 *"Soul Brothers"* LP The first of two star sessions with Ray trading lines with pianist and vibes player Milt Jackson of the Modern Jazz Quartet.

1958 *"Soul Meeting"* was second LP featuring Ray sparring with Milt.

1959 *"The Genius of Ray Charles"* was his first entry in the pop chart reaching No. 17 followed by his first pop hit single *"What'd I Say."*

1960 A move to ABC Records under a lease-tape agreement gave Ray virtual control over his recordings and guaranteed that the rights would revert to him after the contract expired. The first fruit of this deal was the No.1 single *"Georgia on My Mind."*

1961 *"Genius Plus Soul Equals Jazz"* LP featured Basie sidemen (and included single *"One Mint Julep"*) with arrangements by Quincy Jones.

1961 *"Hit the Road Jack"* becomes Ray's second No. 1 single.

1961 *"Ray Charles and Betty Carter"* album of duets charts.

1961 Ray picks up his first Grammy Award.

1962 *"Modern Sounds in Country and Western Music Volume 1"* becomes his only No.1 album and provides the No. 1 pop and R&B hit single *"I Can't Stop Loving You"* (a cover of the Don Gibson song).

1962 *"You Don"t Know Me"* and *"You Are My Sunshine"* are both Top 10 singles.

1962 *"Modern Sounds...Vol 2"* charts at No. 2 in the LP chart.

1963 *"Ingredients In A Recipe For Soul"* repeated its predecessor's success charting at No 2.

1963 Ray keeps his presence felt in the pop singles chart with *"Busted"* and a cover of Hank Williams' *"Take These Chains From My Heart."*

1966 Ray picked up a pair of Grammys for the single *"Crying Time."*

1970 *"My Kind Of Jazz"* LP marked a return to form. Released on Ray's own label Tangerine.

1973 *"Jazz Number II"* LP

1973 *"Ray Charles Live"* LP charts

1976 Ray and Cleo Laine take the parts of Gershwin's downtrodden lovers for a studio recording of *"Porgy and Bess."*

1985 *"Friendship"* LP featured Ray duetting with country music legends.

1987 *"From The Pages Of My Mind"* was universally panned as ill-conceived Nashville schlock.

1993 *"My World"* was a star session featuring celebrity fans Eric Clapton and Billy Preston.

A from-the-wings view of "the Genius" at the piano during the 1962 Comblaine La Tour Jazz Festival in Belgium.

48 june christy

June Christy, "the Queen of Cool," possessed a voice that effortlessly evoked the early 1950s, an era of apparent optimism underscored with apprehension. Her voice had a grainy, arid wispiness, which seemed to come through a smoky haze to make a personal plea to the listener. And when it did, what red-blooded male could resist?

June was born Shirley Luster on November 20, 1925, in Springfield, Illinois. Her initial appearances with local bands were billed under the name Sharon Leslie, a name she kept until she moved to Chicago in 1938 in search of fame.

Her big break came seven years later when she was asked to replace Anita O'Day as featured vocalist in the Stan Kenton Orchestra, possibly because at that early stage in her career she sounded a dead ringer for O'Day. The tight, turn-on-a-dime dynamism and power of Stan the Man's big band proved an ideal setting for June's self-possessed and commanding personality.

During her two years with Kenton, she romanced and married Stan's tenor sax soloist Bob Cooper, developed her own style and recorded several hits, including "And Her Tears Flowed Like Wine," the Latin-flavored "Tampico," and "Shoo-Fly Pie," before leaving to pursue a solo career.

The appeal of swing was losing its momentum by the late 1940s, and June was keen to carve herself a niche of music history as a hip singer of the up and coming "cool" school. To this end she teamed up with one of the most creative arrangers of the day, Pete Rugolo, an ex-colleague from the Kenton band with whom she recorded a run of nine albums for the Capitol label.

The best of those long players, "Something Cool" (1954) and "The Misty Miss Christy" (1956), were remarkably consistent in terms of quality and were years ahead of their time in terms of both vocal styling and arrangements. Both albums, along with "June—Fair and Warmer!" (1957) made the American Top 20 best-selling album charts.

Her laid-back delivery lent a fashionable emotional detachment to the slower numbers, which almost turned some of the tracks into art songs, while on the up-tempo tracks she rode the melody with a restive, almost gleeful bounce. And although she was well established as a solo artist by the early 50s, she continued to answer Kenton's call to record with his new outfits. She even found time to tour with Britain's top big band, the Ted Heath Orchestra (with Bob Cooper as a guest soloist), but was becoming increasingly reluctant to leave her husband and young daughter in California for life on the road.

Having charmed the cognoscenti and topped the prestigious *Downbeat* magazine poll as Best Female Jazz Singer six years in succession, June Christy spent much of the 50s concentrating on enlarging her audience by recording more commercially oriented albums. Her gamble paid off with a hit single, "My Heart Belongs To You," but her reputation rests with the two early Capitol albums, which are essential additions to any self-respecting jazz lover's CD collection.

A by-product of the cool jazz movement that was spawned on America's West Coast—and of which husband Bob Cooper was a leading name—June Christy, the undisputed Queen of Cool, retired from the scene in the early years of the 60s before finally abdicating her throne on June 21, 1990, aged 65.

The following interview presented in the form of a personal address by Ms. Christy appeared on the eve of her appearance at the Festival Hall with the Ted Heath band, April 5, 1958.

I WON'T RECORD RUBBISH !

I'm calling this my first visit to London. I hesitate to even mention the one hour spent in London in 1953, when I was working with the Kenton Orchestra.

It's especially thrilling to be working again with Ted Heath and the boys—this time on their home ground.

Ted has a great band. It's commercial, but all his music is in fine taste. Most of the present-day popular music is so horrible that it really shouldn't be called music. It's actually just some kind of a product.

However, I'm very optimistic for the future. I think they've finally reached the bottom of the barrel. A short while ago I couldn't even contemplate the Top 10. Now there are often one or two quite good things there.

A while back I did some things I didn't believe in. I thought it my duty to go along with the suggestions at Capitol. Truthfully, no one was more glad than I that they didn't sell.

I've been so fortunate at Capitol to have Bill Miller working on my recordings. I'm allowed complete freedom.

No one expected the "Something Cool" LP to sell outside the jazz field. But it did—extensively. Our subsequent albums have been in the same vein.

Now, I'm not looking for any single hits and I wouldn't lower my musical standards to get one.

Sarah and Ella are in the jazz field, too, of course, but they sell to the pop market just the same. Ella has always been my idol. Every singer just has to admit that.

In the earliest days, Anita O'Day influenced me a lot, too. I was often accused of copying her. I didn't consciously. However, when I listen to my old records I think I may have done. I have always wanted to sound like myself, but sometimes, in the beginning, that's very difficult.

Talking of my favorites. I must mention Chris Connor, too—I think she's wonderful.

People have often asked me if it was difficult singing with Kenton because the vocal backgrounds were often loud and involved. You know, I never even thought about it. I was such a fan of Stan's and the music. I was young and inexperienced and so utterly thrilled to be with the band.

Pete Rugolo has done the writing for all my albums so far. Pete, I respect and love dearly. We feel so much the same musically. I never even make suggestions to Pete.

However, "Coop" [husband Bob Cooper] will do the arrangements for my next album. I'm a fan of his, too!

I'm always being told there are so few new jazz singers. It seems most potential jazz vocalists go into the ultra-commercial field where there's more money. Johnny Mathis is a good example. Furthermore, with so few big bands in the United States these days there are no training grounds.

While in England I'm hoping to hear some of the British singers and musicians. If there are other musicians as great as those in the Ted Heath band, I'm in for a treat.

June Christy, pausing during rehearsal for her opening at London's Cool Elephant in late 1964, was interviewed by Max Jones about her plans for 1965.

MISTY MISS NOW PLAYS IT COOL

"I wish I could think of something to tell you, some burning ambition, but really I don't have one. I wish I had more ambition. I guess I am a contented singer.

"I'm here for two weeks, but this was a last-minute panic thing. Long ago I realized that fate is fate. If we're going to open we will. It's useless to worry. Anyway, I'm delighted to have Victor Feldman with me.

Right: The white gardenia look, most associated with Billie Holiday, was popular with many singers, film stars, and fashion-conscious women generally in the 1940s.

"I'll work through February, then spend time at home. In the spring, I'll go out again. That's the pattern."

Meanwhile, carpenters, electricians, and cleaners toiled like beavers to ready the Cool Elephant for opening time. In the middle of these operations, June Christy worked over "It Don't Mean A Thing" and "Remind Me" with pianist Victor Feldman, drummer Allan Ganley, and Spike Heatley on bass. They did open, and Ganley said working with June and Victor was "a gas."

"With a husband [tenorist Bob Cooper] and child like mine, I don't need an ambition. Often I envy the entertainer who just can't wait to go on. I wish there was little more of the ham in me.

"I'm not like that. Frankly, I always feel a bit of stage fright. Except for once maybe. We made an interesting tour on the coast with a bunch called 'Stars For Freedom.' There was a cause behind it, you know.

"It was a lot of fun, and I finally got to sing with the Basie band. No, I never had, and I almost didn't this time. The promoters had me fixed to work with another group, and I was so disappointed.

"Then, as we were starting, Basie came to me and said: 'You sing with the band, of course.' And I did. It was such a ball.

"Luckily, I had my arrangements from the 'Big Band Specials' album, and we did things like Shorty Rogers' marvelous arrangement of 'Prelude To A Kiss' and my husband's 'My Shining Hour.'

"I think this was the first time I had no stage fright. It was all gone. All I wanted to do was sing, and I never enjoyed myself more. Of course it spoils you for life."

June, and husband Bob Cooper, are inveterate record listeners. What is she currently appreciating on the hi-fi rig?

"Basie, naturally. I would love to make an album with the Count. And the good singers—like Ella and Sarah. The same people really I've liked for years.

"One of my favorite things just now is that album by Clark Terry with the Oscar Peterson Trio. It's my present getting-up record. That crazy vocal of Clark's, 'Mumbles.' It starts the day right for me."

On past visits, Miss Christy has proved a stern critic of the contemporary scene. Does she find things changed?

"No, the same is still true. Not enough places featuring good, swinging music, and not enough good new songs being written. It's hard to find them. It's still easier to unearth good old ones, and I'm always doing it.

"We came up with a fine one in 'Remind Me,' a beautiful tune. With these obscure songs, it's like singing a new one—if there were new ones of that quality.

"I've been called an album singer, and it is basically true. Until the market changes, it's kind of impossible for me to move toward it because I'd have to sing things that are against my principles for a start.

"Songwriters are not too interested in writing good, intelligent songs. It's so much easier to write a piece of junk and you know there's a waiting market for it.'"

"Something Cool" is still June's best-selling LP, and she says it is astounding to her that, old as it is, the sales keep up so well. As for the nicknames, based on "Cool" and "Misty," that hang on to her, June is not in favor.

"Handles," she says, "are not necessary any more. And that's a good thing. They don't seem to make any sense to me."

Below: June Christy relaxing in 1951, in the days when smoking was almost *de rigeur* rather than taboo.

key recordings

1945	Hit single *"Tampico"* with Stan Kenton Orchestra makes No. 4 in US charts, a million-seller.
1946	*"Shoo Fly Pie"* single charts at No. 8.
1948	*"How High the Moon"* third single entry at No. 27.
1949	*"Nat Meets June"* LP with Metronome All Stars.
1950	*"Shorty Rogers with Kenton and Christy"* LP with top trumpet star Rogers.
1953	*"My Heart Belongs to You"* is another US hit single.
1954	*"Something Cool"* LP, the title track written by Christy's friend Billy Barnes, makes US album chart.
1955	*"Duet"* album with Stan Kenton.
1956	*"The Misty Miss Christy"* LP featuring top session men Maynard Ferguson and Shelly Manne, is her second entry in the best-selling album lists. *"This Is June Christy"* LP.
1957	*"June—Fair and Warmer"* LP, her third chart album, all three produced by Pete Rugolo.
1959	*"The Song Is June"* LP. *"June Christy Recalls Those Kenton Days"* LP.
1960	*"Cool School"* LP.
1961	*"Do-Re-Mi"* LP, her only film soundtrack album.
1977	Despite semi-retirement, records *"Impromptu"* album with the Lou Levy Sextet.
1986	Reissue of *"The Best Thing for You"* LP.
1989	*"The Capitol Years"* compiles tracks from 1946–65.

Legend has it that Nat King Cole took to vocalizing reluctantly at the insistence of a drunk who had urged him to "Ssshing Ssshweet Lorraine." The story goes that Nat and his trio were well into their regular all-instrumental set at the Swanee Inn, Los Angeles, one night in 1938 when the pickled punter lurched toward them and made his request. Nat politely refused by saying that none of the group sang, but the drunk returned a few minutes later with the club's manager in tow and Nat was persuaded to oblige. It was the same manager, incidentally, who gave Nat his regal title after having him wear a paper party crown to amuse the customers. Incredibly, the multi-million-selling singer who had been blessed with one of the most expressive and appealing voices of the century, was still being forced to compromise to a certain extent 20 years later. In the following interviews, conducted in 1952, Nat talks about having to choose material to appeal to current public taste, and of the pressure to sustain sales to keep his record company happy.

Born Nathaniel Adams Coles on March 17, 1917, in Montgomery, Alabama, Nat was initially inclined to become a jazz instrumentalist, having wowed his adoring parents by thumping out "Yes, We Have No Bananas" on the family piano at the tender age of two.

When the family moved to Chicago, Nat heard his jazz at source, picking up Earl "Fatha" Hines, Fletcher Henderson, and Louis Armstrong as early influences and evolving his own inimitable piano style by playing in the church where his father was the pastor and his mother led the choir.

Following several false starts fronting big bands, recording for local labels, and undertaking grueling touring revues, Nat finally settled for the more flexible format of a instrumental jazz trio—a much imitated line-up that he helped to popularize.

Nat was an accomplished and innovative pianist whose relaxed, conversational vocal style was initially regarded as an optional extra, the icing on the cake, but when the hits kept coming, the fees grew fatter, and film offers flooded in, Nat found himself recast as a

romantic ballad singer. Female devotees had been heard to murmur that his satin smooth voice was akin to a kiss, and the marketing men at Capitol Records, with whom he had signed in October 1942, were keen to have a cut of the lucrative youth and family market that had been cornered by the crooners. So, in 1948, Nat found himself singing pop ballads such as "Nature Boy" and "The Christmas Song" backed by strings—songs that dismayed the purists but pleased the public. The trio were retained for TV, stage, and supper club dates, but from then on Nat was essentially a solo star.

Subsequent singles, such as "Too Young" and "Mona Lisa" turned gold within months of release, earning Nat the distinction of being the only Capitol recording artist to have more than one hit on the list of all-time best-sellers. Even the advent of Elvis couldn't cramp Nat's style, and he continued to have hits throughout the 1950s, including the evergreens "Unforgettable," and "When I Fall In Love." Years later, the latter was a hit all over again as a simulated duet with daughter Natalie, who had overdubbed her part on the original recording. A posthumous Grammy Award for that recording was the crowning achievement for a supreme song stylist who reigned for over two decades with 78 American hit singles (averaging more than three hits a year) and 24 chart albums between 1944 and 1966.

Nat King Cole died in 1965, but collections of his recordings continue to sell steadily in the face of fads and fashions.

 The first two interviews that follow were conducted in 1952 at a time when Nat King Cole was making the crossover from jazz instrumentalist to vocal star, the third a couple of years earlier when he was still best known as a pianist.

YOU CAN GO A LITTLE COMMERCIAL AND STILL PLAY GOOD JAZZ

"The biggest show of 1951 finished last November. We had a grand time on our closing night, at Johntown, Pennsylvania, after we had spent 77 nights together—and that's a lot of one-nighters, believe me.

"I didn't pay too much attention to the attendance, but the one in Detroit drew about 17,000 or 18,000 people.

"You know I pick my own material to record. That sometimes has its disadvantages. I get chased around by just about everybody and his brother who has written a song "

"Have you written one?"

"I get them from all parts of the country, from all types of people—but usually I use material that the publishers are plugging, because they're the ones with the big money behind them.

"Occasionally I may run into a good one along the way—written by some housewife or someone.

"That's how I picked up a thing called 'Nature Boy.' I look at everything I get, you see, and that one hit me back in 1947.

"This guy brought me the song and left it at the stage door. I looked at it, liked the words, and decided to record it.

"Of course, I didn't know it would be as big as it was. I didn't see that far ahead.

"The others though like 'Mona Lisa,' 'Too Young,' and Unforgettable,' are all things that publishers gave to me.

"Bobby Troup gave me one once that did big things for me a few years ago. He had been traveling to the West Coast by car and he was driving by Route 66, so he wrote the song about it.

"One thing that I want to stress is my part in show business. In case you forget, I used to lead a trio at one time: that was before I started to sell records.

"I was strictly a jazz musician and played only jazz—but selling records became more interesting to me. Some of my fans jumped on me for changing, but they don't really understand my reasons for it.

"After all I'm eating now!

"I don't think there is anyone in the business who likes jazz more than I do, but I prefer to keep to the middle of the road.

"You can still be a little commercial and yet play good jazz.

"I try to please both sides because it's a big business. It's a tough thing, trying to keep to the middle of the road.

"I wish that people would accept jazz as readily as they would accept popular music. But you can't reach more people unless jazz becomes more commercial. I don't think it can be done. People aren't really fully educated to jazz. We, the musicians, are still in the experimental stage. We're not sure how we want to interpret the music—so how can we expect the public to understand?

"Bebop, for instance: when it became the rage, instead of feeding it to the public a bit at a time, boppers tried to shove it down everyone's throats in big doses.

"Naturally, the public resented it; who wouldn't?

"I think the public is paying more attention to ballads than anything else these days. A ballad stays around longer than a novelty song. When it hits it's a big song. My own version of 'Too Young' was a good sign.

"Yes it looks as if the public is getting romantic again.

"I'm glad I love ballads!"

Above: Nat King Cole and the Trio entertain at a party hosted by Frank Sinatra in February 1955; here "Ol' Blue Eyes" sits in for a number.

Left: Nat King Cole in front of adoring fans during a ballroom date in the late 1940s.

NO MORE GIMMICKS TO INVENT—SO LET'S PLAY MUSIC AGAIN

The picture presented by the music business nowadays with all this craze for new sounds and gimmicks, is a very confused one.

Naturally, I try to record what I think is commercial, but basically I love jazz; and, of course, anyone is a little worried and cautious about what is going to happen to the business in the future. It's hard to guess.

The guys like Billy May and Neal Hefti and Woody Herman's new band might be starting a new trend in bringing the people back to music—camouflage style, I would say. Maybe they will bring the public back to the dancing way; that would help things a lot.

I'd really like to see the band business come back, because bringing the band business back will help to create more demand for music itself. I myself would love to go off the general trend that I'm on—but naturally you have to concede with what the public is demanding.

After all, you are working for record companies who are in big business—that's money!

In order to maintain that guarantee (if you have one) and maintain that salary they are paying you, you have to sell records for them. They only look at the sheet to see what's selling—they don't care what's creative or what's the greatest sound. So it really is a confusing business, but I think it will eventually come back to normal again.

We always have to pass through these crises. I remember, for instance, a few years back we were going through a real novelty stage. Everything had to be a real silly novelty.

But now I do notice that some good songs are creeping back in, and a few of the artists that are working hard at it are trying to bring back some more.

For myself, I feel the best thing to do is just to bide our time. I feel I can go sit on the fence and I can go any way the tide goes. But basically my heart is still in jazz—whenever I'm at home, all my records are non-vocal records, for example.

When people come to my house and ask if I have some pop song— I don't have it!

I don't have anything vocal—unless it's sung by Louis Armstrong. They can't understand that!

I'm not throwing slams at any of the pop artists, because, after all I'm one of them myself. I follow a trend of the business.

I'm one of the fortunate guys that started out as a musician and could still go over on the other side again: I think that I could even make a comeback as an instrumentalist if need be.

But I'm hoping to see the music business right, now we have some of the most talented musicians as a whole that we have ever had.

The only thing about it is that they're so good and they're all good. You can't distinguish one from the other, as you could in the old days when Hawkins came out and Lester Young. These guys have come up so that they're even doing him one better on other things. You can't distinguish styles any more.

We can't put our fingers on any individual stylist because I think we have reached our peak right now in inventing sounds; so the best thing for us to do is to settle down and go back to what we were playing and play it good.

The public will wake up to it again eventually, because the public is the most fickle thing around. So it's bound to come back to the ground one of these days!

Below: Nat between takes in the recording studio, photographed by Chuck Stewart.

Below, the first part of a backstage interview with Max Jones and Mike Nevard that appeared on September 23, 1950.

WHY I MADE THE TRIO A QUARTET

"Why did we go 12 years without a drummer?" Nat Cole smiled and leaned back in his chair. "Because with one we'd have looked just like a rhythm section. And when we came on stage people would wait for the rest of the band to appear."

Thus Nat destroyed a misconception that he doesn't like drummers. In fact, he takes the keenest interest in the percussion side of the present Afro-Cuban trend.

"That's why I decided to add bongo to the trio. After all those years I wanted to develop our sound, without too drastic a change, and I felt a bongo player would make out fine. I realized, too, the growing interest in Afro-Cuban rhythms. Bongo and conga drums look, and sound, good without giving the impression of a rhythm section.

"I was lucky enough to get hold of Jack Costanzo, who had just left Kenton, and signed him for a two weeks' tour. Things went well, so I decided to keep him on."

NEW ADMIRERS

"Of course, the change met with a lot of opposition at first. They said we'd lose our individual sound and asked why, after all those years of success, we had to make the trio a quartet.

"My answer was that Jack's drumming would add interest to our beat numbers, and enlarge our scope. As for the ballads—they're still trio numbers. Jack doesn't play in them.

"Pretty soon, the people who cribbed accepted the change, and many admitted it was an improvement.

6 0

Below: Rehearsing for the Royal Command Performance in May 1960, photograph taken for the London *Evening Standard* newspaper.

"We won plenty of new admirers.

"What is not generally known is that the first group I ever formed was a quartet—or it was supposed to be. When the manager of the Los Angeles club hired me, he instructed me to engage three other men. I hired a bass, drums, and guitar, but the drummer didn't show up on opening night. So we played as a trio, and made such a hit that we stayed that way."

LUNCEFORD KICK

"Just before we left the States to come here we recorded a couple of numbers with the Kenton band. One was a vocal, 'Orange Colored Sky,' and the other a mambo, 'Jambo.'

"In the 'Sky' one we start off just like an ordinary trio disk. Then that big Kenton orchestra comes in with a bang—and keeps punching in through the record. I think it is a pretty good effect.

"In 'Jambo' Stan and I both play piano with the band backing. I guess you'll be getting the disk over here soon."

Some other interesting records to expect from Nat were cut only two days before he flew here. These were his first recordings with his wife, Marie Ellington, a former Duke singer.

Nat and Marie (she's changed it now to Maria) did duets on "Get Out And Get Under The Moon" and "Hey Not Now" with a studio orch backing conducted by Pete Rugolo.

"The music is on a kind of Lunceford two-beat kick," Nat explained. "But with unmistakable Rugolo touches here and there.

"It made me think of that great band of Jimmy's. It could really swing. Only the other day, I was playing some Lunceford records. Some of the best, like 'Margie' and 'Swannee River,' were the greatest things.

"I wish we had a band like that in the States right now. We've got about five Millers going around, but no one has brought back the Lunceford style. And there's room for it, now, with the public getting a little tired of bop."

SHELVED BOP

When the bop craze was on, the record companies signed up all the bop talent they could lay their hands on and recorded shoals of sides featuring some of the very best in modern music.

"But now, with most of these sides still on the shelves, the demand has fallen. Mention the word 'bop' to a record executive these days and he's fit to jump out of the window.

"Partly, it's the musicians' own fault.

"They rushed it. If they'd worked it out first, and kind of crept in with a little bop here and a little bop there, stepping it up slowly, things would have gone different."

Above: The legendary Cole Trio in action in a typical nightclub venue in the early 1950s.

key recordings

1940   Recorded four sides for Decca including *"That's All Right"* as the Rogues of Rhythm with Nat's brother Eddie on bass, later reissued as *"The Earliest Recordings"* on Decca Jazz.

1941-5   Regular wartime broadcasts backing singers such as Anita O'Day later compiled for *"The MacGregor Years"* on Music and Arts label.

1942   First national hit *"Straighten Up and Fly Right,"* but there were no royalties for Nat, who had sold the publishing rights for $50 to settle a hotel bill!

1943-6   Sessions with Dexter Gordon and Lester Young later released as *"The Lester Young Trio."*

1945   *"Anatomy of a Jam Session"* LP featuring Cole with Buddy Rich, Charlie Shavers, John Simmons, and Herbie Haymer.

1945-50   Various sessions accompanying the Metronome All-Stars including soloists Dizzy Gillespie and Coleman Hawkins and singers Jo Stafford and Kay Starr.

1946   *"I Love You (For Sentimental Reasons)"* peaks at No 1.

1948   First million-selling single *"Nature Boy"* (US No.1) with Frank DeVol Orchestra.

1950   *"Mona Lisa"* arranged by Nelson Riddle hits No.1.

1951   *"Too Young"* third US No.1.

1951   *"Unforgettable"* stalls at No.14 in the US chart but will become a perennial favorite with Nat's fans.

1956   First chart LP *"Ballads of the Day"* (reissued as *"Close-Up"*).

1957   *"Love Is the Thing"* LP tops US chart.

1958   *"Welcome to the Club"* LP with the Count Basie band (but no Basie for contractual reasons). Later reissued under the title *"Big Band Cole."*

1958   Soundtrack LP to the film *St Louis Blues* in which Cole portrayed W. C. Handy.

1958   Release of the LP *"To Whom It May Concern"* with arrangements by Nelson Riddle.

1962   *"Nat Cole Sings / George Shearing Plays"* includes hit single *"Let There Be Love."*

1965   Nat sings the title song to the Jane Fonda/Lee Marvin comic western *Cat Ballou.*

1978   At the height of the disco boom the compilation *"Golden Greats"* tops the UK charts.

Billy Eckstine was one of the most universally popular and most imitated singers of his day, a seminal influence on successive generations of jazz and soul singers and a central figure in the evolution of jazz during the transition from swing to bop. And yet, inexplicably, he is frequently omitted from lists of the great jazz singers.

Billy was born Billy Eckstein on July 8, 1914, in Pittsburgh, Pennsylvania, but altered the spelling of his surname to avoid confusion with the ragtime pianist Willie Eckstein. He needn't have worried. While still in his teens, Billy was already scaling the ladder, working as a singer and emcee in key clubs around Washington, D.C., Buffalo, and Detroit, and getting himself noticed by all the right people.

In 1938, he made the smart move to Chicago where he joined up with the Earl Hines band and was influential in persuading Hines to hire such luminaries as Charlie Parker and Sarah Vaughan. With Hines, Billy made himself a name as a formidable and compelling ballad singer with an impressive vocal range, inimitable phrasing, and impeccable control of vibrato. But he scored his biggest success with a sultry blues, the surprise hit "Jelly Jelly."

In 1943, he left Hines to go solo and a year later formed his own big band with Dizzy Gillespie as musical director. In the three years that Billy steered the band it served as a showcase for future legends, including Dexter Gordon, Fats Navarro, Miles Davis, Charlie Parker, Art Blakey, and vocalist Lena Horne.

Contrary to Billy's expectations, having such a rich roster of talent in one outfit did not guarantee him success. A series of union disputes frustrated his attempts to record, which in turn limited the band's access to radio and the press. But by 1947, the popularity of big bands was in terminal decline and a new approach was called for.

Billy briefly tried his hand with an septet before striking out as a solo singer in 1949 and being rewarded with a string of Top 10 hits on MGM, including "My Foolish Heart" and "I Wanna Be Loved."

As with Nat King Cole, with whom he has often been compared, Billy became an enormous draw for both black and white audiences once his choice of material became more populist, and some of the jazz elements of his orchestrations were muted in favor of lighter, more mainstream-friendly arrangements. But Billy's vocal tone was richer and more sensual than Nat's, and he was indisputably the more robust and impressive performer. Once dubbed by the press "the Sepia Sinatra," the handsome Eckstine was the nearest a black performer came to achieving the status of bobby-sox idol in the late 1940s.

During the 1950s and 60s Billy recorded his share of sentimental showstoppers, but he would return periodically to make albums with arrangers such as Pete Rugolo to replenish and reaffirm his commitment to his roots.

His long-term working relationship with Sarah Vaughan, which stretched right back to the days of the Earl Hines band, resulted in several fine albums of duets, including "Sarah Vaughan and Billy Eckstine Sing the Best of Irving Berlin," recorded in 1957 and, during the same year, the Top 20 hit single "Passing Strangers," which emerged again as part of a compilation of the same name in 1981.

Six years prior to his death in 1993, the normally ebullient Billy was, somewhat uncharacteristically, speechless to find himself sharing a belated Grammy Award with Benny Carter for their eponymously titled album of duets.

In 1954, *Melody Maker* ran a five-week series of reminiscences by Billy Eckstine. The second article, covering his discovery of Sarah Vaughan, appeared on August 21 of that year.

WHEN SARAH VAUGHAN BEGAN TO SING

I didn't make a record until the year 1939. That was with the Earl Hines band, and the first vocal that meant anything was "Jelly, Jelly." I'll tell you how that one came about.

We used to do a lot of traveling in the South, and down there you had to play plenty of blues. Earl never had a blues singer in the band, so he just used to get up and play the thing on the piano and I sang a whole lot of blues choruses—made them up as I went along.

We were doing a session one day, the time we recorded "I'm Fallin' For You," and we had an instrumental that the recording company didn't like so well. They asked Earl: "Earl, have you got anything more commercial you can do instead? How about the blues?"

We said: "Gee, we don't have something off-hand; maybe we'll use that thing we've been jamming." I reminded Earl that we hadn't any original lyrics for it, and he says: "Go outside and write a lyric while we're trying to cut this thing down to three minutes."

So I went out into the anteroom and wrote off the lyric to this thing we recorded, and called it "Jelly, Jelly." It was really a fill-in, as I say, and we figured nothing's going to happen to it. But the thing sold—I don't know—hell, it's gone almost to a couple of million now.

By this time it is some kind of collectors' item in the States, and regardless of where I go I still have to do it when I'm home. Still got to do "Jelly, Jelly" on all American concerts, because they still ask for it. And it's 14 years old.

Now I must tell you a funny bit about Sarah Vaughan. I got Sarah in the band, you know: found her in an amateur show.

It happened this way.

I had a money order I wanted cashed. It was after five o'clock and there was no place to cash it. Then it dawned on me to go into the Apollo Theater and see Mr. Shiffman, the manager in there.

IT'S BEDLAM!

It was amateur night, and there's something I hadn't done before and haven't done since—go into the Apollo on amateur night.

Believe me, Bedlam is in this joint on amateur night, every Wednesday. You can get water thrown on you . . . anything. So nobody even thinks of going in there.

I don't know why I went into the auditorium; it must have been a stroke of fate.

Anyhow, they said Mr. Shiffman had gone around to Frank's to get something to eat, would be back in a few minutes. So I thought I might as well watch the show while I was waiting.

Well, I'm sitting there watching, when from left field they introduce this little girl, and she's going to sing "Body And Soul." She walks out on the stage, just a little skinny thing with a brown skirt on. It is Sarah, and she's about 17 then.

So help me! When she opened up her mouth I started sliding down in my chair. I couldn't believe this, what I was listening to. Right afterwards I went backstage and grabbed her, said: "Look here, I want to talk to you."

She was just as naïve and scared as she could be: right away she figured somebody was giving her a big deal. So I explained that I wanted to have Earl hear her, and I took her number and everything.

To Earl I said: "I have just left the darnedest thing you ever heard in you life—a girl singer." At that time we had a girl—a very pretty girl—but she couldn't carry a tune in a bucket.

The result was that Earl agreed to go and hear Sarah. She had wrecked the house that night, and the Apollo had given her a week's work. Incidentally, it was with Ella Fitzgerald, who was booked there the

Above: The epitome of
suave, photographed in
1950 in characteristic
shirt—there was even
a "Billy Eckstine" collar
style —and tie.

next week, So she and Ella appear on the same bill—Ella the big star and Sarah the kid, the amateur.

Anyway, Earl says: "Yes, she can sing"—and has her come down to Nola's, where we were rehearsing. Now I had told the band about this little chick, how I had never heard anything like it, and the guys were teasing me.

You see, I have never liked chicks singing, because chicks always try to be cute and they forget about what's happening. I mean, they rarely stop to think: this is music, after all; it isn't television.

NOT KIDDING

So when Sassy comes down to the studio, the band looks at her curiously. It was after we'd finished rehearsing for the day, and the guys were packing up their horns when she came in, looking young and kind of ordinary with her hair up on top. Most of the guys were doubtful, and some of them said: "Man, are you kidding?"

At that time the number one song was "There Are Such Things," that Tommy Dorsey had recorded, with Sinatra singing. Earl sits down at the piano and says: "Do you know this, honey?" And starts playing "There Are Such Things."

Sass took the mike they had in this little recording studio, and started singing. You could see the guys stop their packing to stare at each other. By the time she had finished, all of them were around the piano — looking at the homely little girl who was singing like this, just wailing.

When Earl saw the reaction of all the band, she was in. That's how Sarah came into the band. She hadn't worked professionally before, she'd been singing in churches.

As you know, she plays piano, so Earl had two pianos on the stage, and he'd lock the backs of them together. While he conducted, Sarah would sit up there and play just the chords. Then Earl would bring her down to sing, and, boy, she wrecked everywhere we went.

A STRAIGHT TONE

She was singing about like she does on records, but more straight tone then. Some things were a little cold, because of this straight tone, but she and the boys in the band got together, we got real tight, and she was soon singing beautifully.

Myself, and guys in the band like Shadow Wilson, Bird and Diz, Bennie Harris, and Shorty McConnell, we raised Sarah and showed her practically everything that the music business was about.

Later, when she was in my band, if she came late for a job we didn't bother to fine her. I never would fine Sarah if she was late. I'd turn her over my knee and whip her. She wouldn't often be late after that.

And when she did come in late she looked around cautiously. Because one of us was behind the door to grab her and beat the hell out of her. So Sarah came up as one of the guys, just as a musician.

DIZZY, BIRD, AND THE BIRTH OF BOP (published 9/4/54)

Singing has been the big thing in my life since around 1932, when that particular bee bit me in Washington. The singer that inspired me—probably most of you have never heard him. He was with Don Redman's band way back, and his name is Harlan Lattimore.

THE SINGERS

Latty was just fabulous. To me, he had one of the greatest voices that I've heard since or before. He had a nice, warm sound, and he was a smooth baritone. As I was a kid at school when he came to Washington I used to follow him around like a good dog. Yes, Latty was more or less the guy that inspired me.

6 7

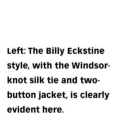

Left: The Billy Eckstine style, with the Windsor-knot silk tie and two-button jacket, is clearly evident here.

Above Right: A rare shot of a tie-less—but still stylish—Eckstine.

Another, slightly late, source of inspiration was Pha Terrell.

Now there's a guy! Pha Terrell was really my buddy, and when he came to town with the Andy Kirk band I used to hang round with him all the time.

Up until Pha came along Negro male vocalists almost always sang blues on records. There wasn't one specializing in ballads.

Pha came up with "Worried Over You," "Clouds," "Until The Real Thing Comes Along," and all those pretty things, and they were so soulful and melodic that he was a definite inspiration also. But Pha's voice was a little higher than mine.

Pha was really wonderful and, aside from singing, man, that cat sure could fight. Boy, he could wail! That's another funny thing: for some weird reason people used to think that all male singers were . . . well, kind of on the lavender side. I used to get in fights all the while to disprove this.

BILLY ECKSTINE REACHES THE FINALE . . . (published 9/11/54)

Now, let's see—what were we talking about last week? Oh, yes. Singers. Which brings me right along to Nat Cole.

First off, I don't think there's anybody around who can read a lyric like Nat does. I love the style Nat has, the really warm feeling.

It may seem funny, but I feel about Nat the same way I do about Louis Armstrong—in singing. I mean, Louis hasn't got "a voice." And fundamentally, Nat hasn't, either. It is the warm sound and soul you hear from the delivery of both of them that makes you say: "This guy is singing hell out of that song."

Nat has that intimate, bedroom style of singing that fractures me. I can truthfully say I have everything he's made, and I like to put his records on when I'm sitting quiet at night.

I mentioned Louis. Now I like modern music: to me, it's so fresh, and it's an inspiration. It's something that is always new, always fresh in your ear. I don't particularly like the stereotyped Dixieland music, but then I don't think of Louis as being an old-time musician.

I think of Louis as being a pillar in music. A person of whom you can say: "Here's the guy that did it." Right now, whatever he plays to me sounds good.

Maybe the modernists won't go along with me on this, but I couldn't care, because I love Louis. And his singing gasses me. He sings some of the hardest songs and makes them sound good.

Sometimes Dizzy plays something of Louis's and another thing I know for a fact: Dizzy idolizes Pops. And Pops digs progressive music. I know he doesn't dig it as far as trying to play it, but I know he likes Diz and Diz admires him.

But for the other singers—I like Perry Como. I like his relaxed style. He doesn't go out to prove anything, but just to sing a song. And then I like Sinatra—the breathing and the technical things Frank does.

BILLIE

Then for the girls, I've already said that I'm no admirer of chick singers, as a rule, and also that Sarah Vaughan is my girl. And Ella Fitzgerald, she can do no wrong for me whatsoever.

Finally, there's Billie Holiday. She can do no wrong to me, either. I can't think of anyone with more soul than Lady Day. Lately they haven't given her many good things to do, but if you want a real styling on a song, there's nobody to out-style Lady.

Below: The great Billy Eckstine Orchestra at a date in Pittsburgh in 1944, with Eckstine conducting, Sarah Vaughan singing, and Charlie Parker in the background on alto sax.

Above: Eckstine poses in Pittsburgh, Pennsylvania, with his brand new 1942 Cadillac convertible.

key recordings

1940 First hit *"Jelly Jelly"* while a member of the Earl Hines band. Other records included *"Skylark," "Water Boy,"* and *"Stormy Monday Blues."*

1944-7 Recordings with the all-star band featuring Charlie Parker and Sarah Vaughan include *"Good Jelly Blues," "Cool Breeze," "Lady Bird,"* and *"Blowing the Blues Away."*

1945 Armed Forces network sessions collected on LP *"Together"* (Spotlight Records).

1949 First solo hits on MGM *"My Foolish Heart," "I Wanna Be Loved,"* and *"I Apologize."*

1957 *"Passing Strangers"* single hit with Sarah Vaughan.

1957 *"Sarah Vaughan and Billy Eckstine Sing the Best of Irving Berlin"* LP.

1958 Release of the big band LP *"Imagination"* featuring a sturdy set of standards with imaginative arrangements by Pete Rugolo.

1960 *"At Basin Street"* with arrangements by Quincy Jones.

1960 *"No Cover, No Minimum"* LP recorded before a Las Vegas audience.

1985 Double disk compilation *"Everything I Have Is Yours"* includes tracks from 1947–57.

1987 Grammy Award winning LP *"Billy Eckstine Sings with Benny Carter."*

Ira Gershwin once remarked that he hadn't realized just how good his songs were until he heard Ella Fitzgerald sing them, while Irving Berlin is known to have badgered Ella to add an album of his tunes to her celebrated songbook series, because he was constantly being teased with her Cole Porter set by his grandchildren.

For almost 60 years, Ella commanded the unreserved respect of the great American songwriters, the critics, the musicians she worked with, and the audiences she entertained, because she was a consummate artist, fully committed to her craft. She was also capable of investing even the most mundane material with a spirit of spontaneity and elegance. Who else could have breathed warmth and sophistication into the children's nursery rhyme"A-Tisket A-Tasket" as she did, and made it sound significant?

Although she was uncomfortable being labeled a jazz singer, Ella's innate sense of harmony combined with her vocal agility, phrasing, shading, and flexibility, singled her out as a singer with swing.

She once summed up her approach to singing by saying, 'You tell it like a beautiful story, and it's always a story that happened to somebody else."

She was born in Newport News, Virginia, on April 25, 1917, but was raised by her aunt in New York City. After winning $25 at an amateur talent contest at Harlem's Apollo Theater in 1934, she auditioned for Tiny Bradshaw, which led to a steady job with his band and some valuable experience. This prepared her for more prestigious engagements with the Chick Webb Orchestra, for whom she made her first recordings. Webb became her mentor and, later, her guardian when her mother died, a gesture she reciprocated by creating what was to be Webb's biggest hit, "A-Tisket A-Tasket."

In gratitude, and because he evidently knew a winner when he heard one, Webb made Ella the focus of his show, a show that she inherited when he died in 1939. But running a band was not for someone of Ella's anxious temperament and congenital shyness, and so, after a short stab at going solo, she entrusted her professional future to producer and promoter Norman Granz, and allowed him to steer her career.

The songbook series was Granz's personal project, although it is doubtful whether he or Ella appreciated the scale of the task they had undertaken. It took almost ten years, from 1956–64, to record the complete cycle, a total of more than 16 hours of music. But the result was the most comprehensive collection of American popular song on record. It earned the unqualified approval of the composers and also had the distinction of being among the first double-disk sets to chart. In addition to paying tribute to George and Ira Gershwin, Ella reinterpreted the classic songs of Rodgers and Hart, Jerome Kern, Harold Arlen, Cole Porter, Johnny Mercer, and Duke Ellington on individual albums, with the collaboration of the cream of arranger/conductors such as Nelson Riddle, Buddy Bregmann, and the Duke himself. Even Irving Berlin finally got the ultimate accolade with which to impress his grandchildren.

Moreover, the series celebrated the supreme artistry of Fitzgerald, whose peerless performances were remarkably consistent and sympathetic to the material, even when the jazz elements were minimal.

The songbook series alone would have secured Ella the status of a cultural institution, but she went on to make dozens of classic recordings with giants of equal stature—such as Count Basie and Louis Armstrong—before ill-health put an end to half a century of peerless performances.

Ella Fitzgerald died from complications brought on by bad circulation and diabetes on June 15, 1996, at the age of 79.

Max Jones interviews Ella prior to her 1963 UK tour.

I DIDN'T ASK FOR THE TAG

"Jazz singer?" Ella Fitzgerald registered a certain resignation, as though she'd heard the question before.

But she indicated that she considered herself to be a singer of jazz and popular songs who didn't ask to be classified too closely.

"I don't care to restrict myself, and fans today don't like a person doing only one thing. What makes me feel bad is writers and people complaining because I'm not doing this or that.

"Just because you sing something they don't like, they say you're not a jazz singer. Well, I didn't ask for the title.

"They put it on you, then expect you to stick by it. If you're not singing fifths and sevenths, you're no longer a jazz singer.

"There's nothing new about me singing popular things. For the past four or five years I haven't been sticking to jazz. And when I did more jazz numbers, fellows were writing: 'How much of "How High the Moon" can you take?'

"But then when I turn to the other things, and try new material, they try to make me resent being commercial.

"I'll tell you how I feel about it. You have different people in an audience, and not all of them like the same music. Some come to hear jazz, others to hear the songbooks."

GIMMICK

"I can feel when they enjoy a song, and I like to please and surprise them. I like doing these unusual things, myself. It isn't just a gimmick when I try 'Loop de loop.' I like mixing things up."

Ella smiled and dabbed her eyes and went on: "But I feel bad when they're putting me down because I'm not hip enough or something. I don't go out just to please one class of audience. You just can't do that any more.

"Take 'Loop de loop,' which I did on my opening show. I didn't put it in as a jazz classic. It's like I thought. I'll do something that's popular

Right: Ms. Fitzgerald wows 'em at the 1967 Newport Jazz Festival.

Above Left: At the birth of bebop, Ella in the early 40s with (right) trumpet pioneer Dizzy Gillespie.

Above: Ella at New York's Downbeat Club in 1949, watched by an appreciative audience that includes Duke Ellington, front center, and, over Duke's left shoulder, clarinet star Benny Goodman.

here. People seemed to go for it, but the critics will say it's commercial. "In Germany, they wanted me to do 'Mack the Knife,' so I learned it. Eventually it went on a single and that became a hit. Actually, it's not a jazz tune but I can swing it.

"How do you know how a tune will sound until you try it? When I sing 'Loop' I don't do it like the original. I swing it and do it my way and I think it's cute."

CONFUSED

"Course, I don't know if you call it jazz. Right now they have so many versions of jazz it's all getting confused. At the moment they even call church music jazz.

"I mean, they're voting for church singers in the jazz poll."

This was a reference to the recent *Melody Maker* Critics' Poll. When Ella first glanced at it, during a rehearsal, she said: "Oh, well, they got tired of me. I lost my title to Sarah."

WORRIER

Then, to the musicians: "Come on fellas . . . you got to put me back in the groove."

On Sunday, discussing gospel and jazz, she added: "I see critics voting for Sister Tharpe and Mahalia Jackson. Well, if they're jazz singers . . . Yeah, they're good singers, but jazz? Well, I ask you?"

Ella is a perfectionist and, I suspect, a chronic worrier. She is minutely concerned with every detail of her performance, responsive to every nuance of her accompaniment and each shifting mood of her audience, and to every criticism.

Most of us, I'm sure, go to marvel at the beauty, the flexibility, and intelligence of her singing, without thinking whether it falls into this category or that. It is somehow typical of Ella to "feel bad" because a few people have criticized her repertoire.

APPALLED

In view of the effort, worry, and nervous strain, and all the subsequent soul-searching that attend each performance. I sometimes wonder why Ella doesn't retire temporarily, or ease off the schedule drastically.

If she were to give up work for a while, how would she interest herself? Ella looked less appalled at the prospect than I'd expected.

"Oh, I'd spend some time at home with my son, Ray Brown Jr. He's at the age when I should be with him, and I'd enjoy that, of course.

"Then, too, I want to do research on songs, look for standards that haven't been done to death, and good songs that perhaps no one has yet recorded."

Ella talked to Maurice Burman early in 1958.

ELLA: "I PREFER BALLADS"

"If you keep the flash bulbs away you'll get a good interview out of Ella. She's scared of them." It was Norman Granz talking as he led me over to Ella Fitzgerald's table in the Dorchester Hotel.

"Miss Fitzgerald," I said to her as I sat down, "on behalf of almost everybody I know, may I thank you for all the wonderful music you have given us."

The photographers had already begun crowding round—I counted 19—and flash bulbs were going continuously not more than a yard away. Ella was rubbing her eyes and looking worried.

We struggled on: "Every girl singer in the world wishes she could sing like you," I said. "What does it feel like to be perfection?"

Below: Ella Fitzgerald in 1955, in front of a microphone that looked decidedly ancient even then!

"I am not perfection. I am far from perfect, but I always try to improve."

"As a matter of fact I've heard you breathe in the middle of a word."

"What!" she exploded. "I've never noticed it—no one's ever told me that before . . ."

"The word is 'gliding' and the record is 'Manhattan.'"

She turned suddenly to the photographers, who were calling out instructions. "I can only do one thing at a time. I can't look in all directions at once and answer questions at the same time. And you," she added, turning to me, "let me finish one question before you ask the next."

FIERCE PRIDE

On stage Ella Fitzgerald is plump, gentle, and cuddly. Off stage she is slimmer, younger-looking, and very alert. She has great dignity and a fierce pride. Her speaking voice has the same magic, tender quality of her singing.

"What do you think of Sarah Vaughan?" I went on.

"I love her. I love Sarah not only as a singer but as a person. What do you think . . ."

She broke in: "I love them all and they're all good in their own fields." In a sing-song voice she went on: "I love Nat, Perry, Frank . . ."

"Billie Holiday?"

"I love her, too, but I hate being asked who my favorite singer is."

She threw her arms out."I love everybody."

"You love everybody and you sing about love. Are you in love?"

DIPLOMATIC

She gave me a challenging look. "Yes, I am. I'm in love with the spring, with my music, and with life—and I think that's what you call being diplomatic. Huh?"

"May I say you look slimmer than when I last saw you."

"Oh, thank you, thank you—that's the sweetest thing you've said today."

She was wearing a dark blue dress, pearl necklace and earrings, and looked strikingly attractive.

Lou Levy came by and said in an assumed English accent: "Hullo, Ella, old girl, welcome to England."

"Hullo, Cholmondley, old boy," she answered.

I started again: "Ella, do you find yourself compromising between your jazz sense and the melody?"

"Not necessarily. I've made an album of Irving Berlin and in some of these tunes we swing it a little. But I prefer ballads because you tell a story more. The fast ones, however, do help to break it up. But you must always make the melody clear."

"You didn't sing the melody in 'How High the Moon,'" I joked.

"I did. I did. What are you trying to do to me? I sang the melody in the first chorus. You're trying to be technical with me and I did sing the melody."

I changed the subject hurriedly. "How do you feel about so many singers copying you?" I asked.

"I feel very honored."

"The HMV people tell me you're going to have a hit in 'Swingin' Shepherd Blues.' It's being released this week."

"I believe I shall be singing it over here. I'll have to relearn it. I'd sure like to have a single—the albums are OK, but I'd like a single hit."

Above: "Jazz At The Philharmonic" visits Sweden in 1952 with, in rehearsal (l to r), Ella, Oscar Peterson, Roy Eldridge, and drummer Max Roach.

Above: Ella in the 1950s during a Norman Granz "Jazz At The Phil" tour, with (l to r) Granz, tenor star Flip Phillips, and clarinet virtuoso Buddy de Franco.

key recordings

1938	First hit *"A-Tisket A-Tasket"* as singer with the Chick Webb orchestra. Ella is later featured singing it in the 1942 Abbott and Costello movie *"Ride 'em Cowboy."*
1940-51	Three hit singles with the Ink Spots including double sided No. 1 *"I'm Making Believe"*/ *"Into Each Life Some Rain Must Fall."*
1946	Calypso-styled solo hit *"Stone Cold Dead In the Market."*
1949	*"Baby its Cold Outside,"* a hit single with R&B saxophonist and bandleader Louis Jordan.
1955	Appeared in the film *Pete Kelly's Blues* which also featured Peggy Lee.
1956	*"Ella Sings the Cole Porter Songbook"* double album charts at No. 15.
1956	*"Ella and Louis"* LP charted at No. 12, featuring Oscar Peterson, Herb Ellis, and Buddy Rich.
1956	Her talent for scatting can be best sampled on *"Party Blues"* with Basie and Joe Williams.
1957	*"Ella Sings the Rodgers and Hart Songbook"* LP.
1957	*"At The Opera House,"* a superlative set from Ella, Oscar Peterson, and the JATP crew in such gems as *"Oh Lady Be Good"* and *"Stompin' at the Savoy."*
1957	The second installment in the series *"Ella Sings the Rodgers and Hart Songbook"* charts at No. 11.
1958	With Louis Armstrong, Ella took the role of Bess for a disk studio recording of Gershwin's popular opera *"Porgy and Bess."*
1958-9	*"Ella Sings the George and Ira Gershwin Songbook"* LP.
1960-4	A series of live LPs *"Mack the Knife—Ella In Berlin," "Ella in Hollywood," "Ella and Basie!"* and *"Hello Dolly."*
1960	*"Mack The Knife"* becomes a single hit, No. 6 in the R&B charts.
1963	*"On the Sunny Side of the Street"* LP with Basie.
1963	*"Ella and Basie"* LP with Quincy Jones at the helm, and Ella in fine form on *"Shiny Stockings"* and *"Dream a Little of Me."*
1963	*"These Are the Blues"* LP with a hand-picked ensemble featuring Roy Eldridge on trumpet.
1965	*"Whisper Not"* LP.
1967	An album of sacred songs, *"Brighten the Corner."*
1973	*"Take Love Easy"* has Ella cruising in low gear with guitarist Joe Pass.
1973	*"Live at Carnegie Hall"* LP.
1983	*"Nice Work if You Can Get It,"* an album of Gershwin duets with André Previn.

The tragic life of Billie Holiday suggests that there is some truth in the old adage that states that you have to have paid your dues to be a great singer. Billie was arguably the greatest jazz singer of them all, "the voice of jazz," to borrow the title of one of her albums. Her vulnerability, alluring sensuality, sincerity, and emotional range of expression from carefree swing to pained resignation irradiated every performance that she gave. There was no artifice in her performance, no contrived stylizing, or empty gestures. The title of her autobiography, *Lady Sings the Blues*, was aptly chosen, but it only told a tenth of the true story, which was that Billie didn't just sing the blues, she lived them.

Billie was born Elinore Harris on April 7, 1915, in Baltimore, Maryland. The illegitimate daughter of jazz guitarist Clarence Holiday, she moved to New York in her teens to escape a life of prostitution in the brothels of Baltimore. She had been a victim of childhood rape and was confined to an institution, after which she seemed destined for a life on the streets. However, the offer of work as a singer in the night clubs of Harlem held out a glimmer of hope. There she acquired her nickname "Lady," which was conferred on her by the other girls, who sneered at her resentment at having to pick up tips from the tables between her legs. But Billie kept her innate dignity and developed a talent for improvisation to alleviate the boredom of having to sing the same song at each table, night after night.

Legendary producer John Hammond discovered her in 1933 and produced her first sessions with bandleader Benny Goodman. Hammond had been struck by Billie's "exquisite phrasing," and her ability to reinterpret songs in a unique and original fashion, qualities that were to produce some of the finest jazz recordings of the era when she was teamed two years later with pianist Teddy Wilson, trumpeter Buck Clayton, and saxophonist and soul mate Lester Young. Together, this coterie of close friends recorded over a hundred sides between 1935 and 1942 for Vocalion and Brunswick, who were releasing singles not only for the consumer trade but also for the lucrative jukebox market.

During this productive period, Billie also toured with Count Basie and then with Artie Shaw (who became her lover), and was deeply affected by the racial prejudice she was to encounter traveling as the first black vocalist in an all-white band.

She then struck out in 1939 as a soloist, scoring great success with the anti-racist song "Strange Fruit" and the equally moving "God Bless the Child," which became her unofficial theme song. A move to Decca in 1944 found Billie in a lush setting with full orchestra, and recast in the role of popular ballad singer for tracks such as "Lover Man," "Porgy," and "That Old Devil Called Love." But by then her voice was already beginning to show signs of strain, and her performances were increasingly erratic. A heroin habit was largely to blame, but her private life, too, was in turmoil. She had been ill-used by a succession of men in whom she had vainly searched for a husband/father figure, and thereafter her hunger for security and affection became focused on drugs. Her addiction led to a spell in jail, where she took "the cure," but after her release she became convinced that the public was only interested in her because of her notoriety.

Her latter years produced some sporadically fine recordings for Verve, but she never recaptured her early passion. She died in a New York hospital aged 44 on July 17, 1959, from a fatal cocktail of alcohol and drugs. The final act of her tragic life saw her arrest for possession of narcotics while she lay in the hospital on her deathbed.

In an article published February 13, 1954, subtitled "Harlem's Royal Family," Billie Holiday talked about her nickname, Lester Young, and much more during a press conference held at the start of a British 0tour.

LADY DAY SAYS: LESTER YOUNG GAVE ME MY TITLE

After three weeks of touring in Scandinavia, Germany, Switzerland, Holland, and France with Leonard Feather's Jazz Club USA, Billie Holiday arrived in London on Monday.

She was accompanied by her husband and manager Louis McKay, and pianist Carl Drinkard (Feather followed them in on Tuesday). With them on the plane from Paris was dancer-vocalist Taps Miller, here to join the Jack Parnell "Jazz Wagon" Variety show.

From the airport, Billie went straight to her hotel in Piccadilly to meet the press. Tired, and obviously anxious to relax, she was closely questioned by lay press reporters about "her trouble" and the fact that she is not now permitted to work in New York cabaret.

Patiently, Billie explained: "I can't work in any place in New York that sells whisky. Why whisky? Well, it's a city ordinance or something. I guess they're stuck with it.

"I'm trying to get my police card back. You know, I'm not the only one. Some kids've been in trouble two or three times; they are still working. So why pick on me? Somebody's got a hand in it, somewhere, some kind of politics. That's what I'm squawking about."

Cutting another question short, she said: "No, I don't think it's because I'm a Negro, or anything like that. I just don't dig it. I guess someone has to be the goof."

UNFAIR DEAL

Louis McKay added that getting back into New York cabaret could mean upward of $75,000 a year. Billie said: "It's not just the dough, it's the principle of the thing. To me, it's unfair."

As the questioning proceeded, a tired and puzzled Billie began to look restless; her answers became more laconic.

"You mean the authorities won't forget your trouble?" asked one daily newspaper.

"Seems like it," Billie answered.

"The TV program that was put on about you," said another. "I

understand it didn't help you much."

"Didn't do any harm," Billie assured him.

"I suppose all your friends are still fighting for you, Miss Holiday," came another question.

"You know, we don't talk about it, we forget about it," said Miss Holiday meaningly.

Deciding it was time for rescue, the *MM* asked Billie how she came by her name Lady Day.

"Now that's been going on since around 1938," she told us. "I was given that title by Lester Young, the President. I was with Basie's band for a time, and Lester used to live at home with my mother and me.

"I named him the President, and he named me Lady and my mother Duchess. We were the Royal Family of Harlem." Billie laughed at this, drank a little Scotch and suddenly looked offended. "I hate it without ice," she said.

So while somebody rang down for ice-water, Lady Day mused over Lester Young:

THE PRESIDENT

"Yes, he was the President and I was Vice-President (pronouncing it Presi*dent*). I used to be just crazy about his tenor playing, I wouldn't make a record unless he was on it. He played the music I like, he didn't try to drown the singer. Teddy Wilson on piano was the same, and the trumpet player Buck Clayton."

Opposite Left: A white gardenia in her hair was Lady Day's trademark through much of her career.

"But Lester's always been the President to me; he's my boy—and with him I have to mention Louis Armstrong and Bessie Smith. Many's the whipping I got for listening to their records when I was a child.

"I used to run errands for a madam on the corner. I wouldn't run errands for anybody, still won't carry a case across the street today, but I ran around for this woman because she'd let me listen to all Bessie's records . . . and Pops's record of 'West End Blues.'

"I loved that 'West End Blues' and always wondered why Pops didn't sing any words to it. I reckoned he must have been feeling awful bad. When I got to New York, I went to hear him at the Lafayette Theater. He didn't play my blues, and I went backstage and told him about it.

I guess I was nine years old then. Been listening to Pops and Bessie ever since that time. Of course, my mother considered that kind of music sinful; she'd whip me in a minute if she ever caught me listening to it. In those days, we were only supposed to listen to hymns, or something like that."

By this time, most of the daily press—baffled by the Pops and Presidents—had stolen out. Billie didn't seem worried by their departure. "Some of those guys were getting me a little salty," she said. "I didn't come three thousand miles to talk about that. It's ended."

Before leaving, we asked Billie when her British visit would be over.

"I'll be here until Tuesday, I reckon, after that I'm not sure," she said. "We've been offered so many jobs—Paris, Africa, even some Variety in England. Daddy"—here she looked across at husband Louis— "hasn't made our plans yet, but we have a good offer back home."

BILLIE'S DATES

Britain's legion of Lady Day enthusiasts can see her at Manchester tonight (Friday), Nottingham tomorrow, and the Albert Hall, London, on Sunday. Right after the Albert Hall concert, she will appear at the Flamingo, Leicester Square, her sole jazz club date.

Billie says she'll be singing many of her old recorded favorites—including "Porgy," "Strange Fruit," "Billie's Blues," "Fine and Mellow," and "I Only Have Eyes for You"—and some songs she has recorded more recently for Mercury, like "Blue Moon" and "Yesterdays."

On the way out of the hotel, we said goodbye to Billie's pianist, Carl Drinkard. He joined Billie in Washington in 1949, his first recording with her was "Crazy He Calls Me."

Said Carl: "I've been with Lady nearly five years. You know something? Her singing still amazes me."

The following week the *Melody Maker*'s venerable jazz writer Max Jones ran a piece "on the road" in Manchester.

MAX JONES SPENDS A HOLIDAY WITH BILLIE

When Billie Holiday stepped onto the stage of the Free Trade Hall last Friday, the applause must have frightened the porter in the Midland Hotel up the street.

The almost unbelievable had happened. Lady Day was behind a Manchester microphone, wearing a black dress with a gold thread in it, diamond necklace and earrings, and a patch of silver-sprayed hair a little to one side—where the gardenias used to be pinned.

She smiled slightly in ackowledgment, then rocked into "Billie's Blues," then a fastish "All of Me," a beautiful "Porgy," "I Cried for You" (which began slowly, then whipped up), and a weird "Them There Eyes' on which she and pianist Carl Drinkard seemed to travel separate ways.

Above: Billie Holiday in 1952, photographed by Bob Willoughby.

8 2

Right: California during the early 50s, Billie performs one of the few twelve-bar blues songs in her repertoire, the self-penned "Fine And Mellow."

THE BEST SINGER

This was really it—for me and, I'm sure, most of the 2000 people there. I had gone into the hall with the conviction that Billie was the best lady singer still on the jazz scene. So the performance was a confirmation rather than a discovery.

The only doubt I had in advance of the date was whether she could possibly sound as good as she does on records. The answer, in the round, is yes, although one tends (illogically) to be disappointed when she departs from a cherished interpretation of a classic song like, say, "Porgy" or "Fine and Mellow."

And to back up the feeling and individuality of Billie's voice and method are a striking appearance and most uncorny stage manner.

Not for Billie the hammy showmanship characteristic of so many visiting "vocal stars."

FINAL BLOW

As a singer, she grew famous, and as a singer she knocks us out—with that personal phrasing and timing; uncanny control of pitch, and the emotion her voice conveys—although her appearance, as I say, is what administers the final blow.

On stage she looks calm and dignified; but she also looks warm and sounds warm, and her whole attitude seems spontaneous and very, very hip. (I can think of no English word that describes her as well.)

At Manchester she was very happy until the microphone gave up after "Blue Moon," her eighth number. She then gave us "My Man" unaided by electricity (most wonderful it sounded from the front rows), then retired without doing the encores, "I Only Have Eyes for You" and "Strange Fruit."

All the same, it had been a fine concert. Drinkard, Tony Kinsey, Sammy Stokes, and—for certain numbers—trumpeter Dickie Hawdon, tenor saxmen Don Rendell and Tommy Whittle, and the baritone player Ronnie Ross, in my view gave Billie Holiday the best support she got on her short tour.

And Billie's own performance moved me more than any of her others—perhaps because it was my first Holiday concert; perhaps because the hall was good, the crowd was dead silent, and I was positioned to catch every vocal inflection and every gesture of face, hand, and shoulder.

Now and again she announced a song, looking surprised the first time when applause broke out before she had reached the title. Afterwards she told me:

"I never speak on the stage, I once did 36 songs at Carnegie Hall and didn't say a damn word. I just felt happy with this English audience . . . diggin' everything I was doing. I guess they wanted to hear my talking voice as well as my singing."

The idea of this seemed completely new to Billie.

We went back to the hotel and celebrated Lady Day's first British concert. Carl Drinkard, Doug Tobutt (of the Harold Davison office), and the Flamingo's Jeff Kruger were there, and later Harold Pendleton came over from the hall, full of regrets for the faulty mike.

"Forget about it," said Billie. "That was such a sweet little guy who came out and apologized and brought me another mike . . ." (this one didn't work either) ". . . he apologized so much I felt sort of as if I'd ruined his show. When you go back be sure to tell him I love him."

Above: Billie Holiday looking considerably older than her forty years in 1955.

Above: Backstage in New York City, 1948, with her pet Great Dane "Mister."

key recordings

1933 First recordings *"Your Mother's Son-In-Law"* and *"Riffin' the Scotch"* with Benny Goodman.

1935 Records the first of 100 jukebox sides with Lester Young, Buck Clayton, and Teddy Wilson, including *"The Very Thought of You,"* *"Them There Eyes,"* and *"I Cover the Waterfront."*

1935-9 Albums *"Fine and Dandy,"* *"Of Thee I Swing,"* *"Warmin' Up,"* *"Too Hot for Words,"* *"Blue Moon,"* and *"Moments Like This."*

1938 *"Any Old Time"* is the only memento of Billie's stint with Artie Shaw, recorded by Victor to compensate Billie for their refusal to record *"Strange Fruit."* B-side to the song is by Billie herself, *"Fine and Mellow."*

1939 Billie records the bitter anti-lynching song *"Strange Fruit."*

1944 *"Lover Man"* sets Billie among lush strings and marks her transition from jazz to popular singer with Decca. It was her only chart entry. Other standards to get the new treatment include *"That Old Devil Called Love"* and *"Crazy He Calls Me."*

1949 Records duets with Louis Armstrong, including *"My Sweet Hunk o' Trash."*

1949 *"Tain't Nobody's Business if I Do"* recorded in answer to her arrest for possession of opium.

1953 She signs with Norman Granz's Verve label and the following year makes her first tour of Europe and appears at the Newport Jazz Festival.

1956 *"Carnegie Hall"* live concert LP captures Billie in good voice and in full command of her material.

1957 *"Songs for Distingué Lovers"*—Billie world-weary but in distinguished company including Jimmy Rowles, Ben Webster, and Harry Edison.

1958 *"Lady in Satin,"* a controversial set in that Billie is clearly past her best and yet she is intent on giving the songs her all; the contrast between smooth strings and Billie's hoarse rasp is almost too painful to hear on occasions. A strangely compelling set.

1959 The eponymous *"Billie Holiday"* on MGM, completed just weeks before her death.

Peggy Lee prides herself on being perceived as the personification of professionalism. During her 50-year career she settled for nothing less than the best, which often meant cherry-picking the cream of the world's session musicians to record and perform with, demanding that stages be rebuilt to afford her a grand entrance and even flying a lyricist from Hollywood to New York to write a few new verses for a club date. But these were not the melodramatic gestures of a prima donna, rather the expression of a determined perfectionist for whom second best would be second rate.

Peggy was born on May 26, 1920, in Jamestown, North Dakota, with the rather unpromising name of Norma Delores Egstrom. Her first big break came in 1941 when she was spotted singing with a vocal trio at a Chicago hotel, and was recruited by Benny Goodman on the strength of her ability to sing the blues with a veneer of sophistication. For two years she stamped her individuality on songs such as "I Got It Bad and That Ain't Good," "Blues in the Night," "The Way You Look Tonight," and the number one "Somebody Else Is Taking My Place," before leaving the band to marry Goodman's guitarist Dave Barbour.

It had been her intention to retire to suburban domesticity with her husband, but after a year she was tempted back to the studio, initially to record for Capitol (1945–51), then Decca (1952–56), before finally settling down with Capitol through the 1960s.

During these years, she racked up 40 major hits, including several songs co-written with her husband, namely "It's a Good Day" (1947) and the number one hit "Mañana"(1948).

Her translucent tone, and yearning, teasing sensuality, hid a fiercely independent personality that surfaced at several key moments in her career. One notable occasion occurred in 1952 when Peggy was keen to record "Lover" in an impressionistic arrangement penned by Gordon Jenkins, who was noted for his work with Judy Garland, Nat King Cole, and Frank Sinatra. Capitol tried to dissuade her, and so she turned instead to Decca, who helped make it one of her most memorable hits.

Another occurred in the 1980s, when she squared up to the might of the Walt Disney empire who were intent on reissuing *Lady and the Tramp* on video without offering an extra payment for her contribution to the original film. Peggy had provided the voice of Lady, the leading canine character. Refusing to be intimidated or taken for granted, Peggy took the corporation to court and won a substantial settlement.

Her other forays into movies had included the banal *Mr. Music* (1950) with Bing Crosby, a schmaltzy remake of *The Jazz Singer* (1955) with Danny Thomas in the Jolson role, and the atmospheric *Pete Kelly's Blues* (1955), for which her performance as an alcoholic torch singer brought her an Academy Award nomination. The latter also saw her in the company of Dixieland legends Matty Matlock and Dick Cathcart.

Her track record in the studio was more consistent than her film career. One of the highlights was the certified classic "Black Coffee," a 10" album featuring trumpet virtuoso Pete Candoli and piano maestro Jimmy Rowles, which was subsequently reissued with extra tracks to make a 12" LP. The title track, later covered by Otis Redding, was one of many self-penned standards that helped to rate her as one of the most bankable song-writers in the business. Others included collaborations with Quincy Jones ("New York City Blues") and Duke Ellington ("I'm Gonna Go Fishin'").

And then there were classy albums like "The Man I Love" with Sinatra conducting, "Jump For Joy" with arrangements by Nelson Riddle, "Beauty and the Beat" with pianist George Shearing, and "Mink Jazz" with Benny Carter. But the track that will be forever associated with Peggy was her imaginative reworking of Little Willie John's R&B sizzler "Fever," which remains perennially popular and a cornerstone of her concert repertoire.

Her contribution to popular music was celebrated at an all-star concert in 1994 which featured kd lang and Cleo Laine, while Peggy Lee herself continues to record and perform into the 1990s. Even ill-health could not deter her from appearing with the Brandenburg Symphony Orchestra at London's Royal Festival Hall in 1994 for a sell-out concert. So, true to character, she took to the stage in a wheelchair.

A 1961 interview by Ren Grevatt in New York.

MOST OF TEENAGE MUSIC MAKES ME SICK

Miss Talent—Peggy Lee, that is—was perched on the edge of the stage singing "Travelin' Light" in her whisperingly provocative way when I walked into New York's Basin Street East club.

It was an afternoon rehearsal—the afternoon before her triumphant return engagement in the Manhattan boîte, a spot where, one year before, she had broken all records.

BILLIE HOLIDAY

"Travelin' Light" is just one part of her new act. But it's an important part, for it's a tribute to the late, great Billie Holiday.

"I never knew 'Lady Day' very well," Peggy confessed, "but I knew her well enough to realize her greatness. She was a wonderful artist.

"I'm a little timid about trying to do her songs, but I want people to enjoy them all over again, just as I do.

"I'm terribly sick of so much of the kind of music the kids are getting today. It's so unmusical and unfeeling when you compare it with the music of Billie or Ray Charles.

"My 17-year-old daughter Nicki introduced me to the music of Ray Charles. He's so far above the run-of-the-mill rock'n'roll.

"He's the blues. He's real down-to-earth rhythm and blues. I give him so much credit for teaching our kids something real and authentic about music.

"I've put together a sort of medley of Ray Charles in my act, too, and when I don't do my Lady Day group, I do the Ray Charles numbers. There's so much feeling and soul in them."

Ranging on other topics of interest, Miss Lee revealed a dislike of country music, and her own identification as a band vocalist. For Frank Sinatra, however, she had only praise.

COUNTRY MUSIC

"I know a lot of people think country and western music is wonderful," she asserted. "I don't. Maybe it's because I was raised in North Dakota and, as a kid growing up, I had a steady diet of it. I got sick of it. I like something that swings a little more.

"Everybody reminds me that I was once a band singer with Benny Goodman. Those were great days, of course, and I enjoyed them. But now I'm something else. I want to feel I'm something on my own, that I've made a contribution myself. That's how I want people to think of me."

FRANK SINATRA

I asked Miss Lee to comment on reports she would one day join Reprise Records, Frank Sinatra's new label. "This is the first I've heard of such a story," she remarked. "I can only say that I have a lot of admiration for Frank. When I was between contracts at Decca and Capitol, I did an album with him conducting the band and producing.

"All I can say is, it was a pleasure. And, although some people thought it was a fake, Sinatra did conduct, and he did a terrific job."

Right: A young Peggy Lee in the studios of Capitol Records in Hollywood on April 10, 1946.

The lady who had a great hit with the low down blues "Fever," who recently was a co-writer with Duke Ellington of "Goin' Fishin'," and who would love one day to write the score of a Broadway show, is coming to Britain for her first time as a performer.

"I'll be in California for Nicki's graduation, and then we'll go to Britain in July," she told me. "I've waited this long because I've always wanted to mix business with pleasure. I want to look over everything.

"We're looking forward to our trip, to singing for our friends in London and seeing Europe. It's going to be a great experience."

The following interview by Leonard Feather appeared in 1968.

PEGGY TRIES SOME NEW WINE IN NEW BOTTLES

For the seekers of nirvana in Nevada, she is the music world's blonde contribution to American sex symbolism.

For the few remaining night club owners who can still afford to lure her away from Beverly Hills, she is Miss Standing Ovation of 1968.

For television producers, she is one of those rare women who can conjure up color on a black-and-white screen.

While the music around her has changed with frenzy and fury, Peggy Lee has stood fast, a cool, calm area in the eye of a rocking, rolling hurricane.

When the storm showed signs of settling, she took her good time before deciding on a new direction. She had heard too many of her contemporaries mindlessly jumping aboard the youth market band wagon, the Teenville Trolley, desperately seeking the fastest route to the top of the charts.

Left: Peggy in low-cut gingham at a 1953 nightclub date at the Nevada resort spot, Lake Tahoe.

Below: A much-used 1961 publicity shot from Capitol Records of a mink-clad Miss Lee.

Peggy Lee continued to make records of quality in her own style and tradition, the ballads soulful, the rhythm songs pulsating in her jazz-trained manner, the old-time tunes embellished with an almost burlesque sort of Mae West zest.

Then, a few weeks ago, the word went forth that Madame Mañana had become Miss Now; that authority for all her recordings would be delegated to Charles Koppelman and Don Rubin, two young men who have fashioned settings for the likes of Gary Lewis and the Playboys, the Lovin' Spoonful, and the Turtles.

The other day, trim and composed, speaking in the even tones that sometimes sound as though she is about to break into laughter over some hidden joke, Miss Lee explained her new project.

"These are two very successful producers. No, they're not teenaged millionaires; I guess they're just plain old 28-year-old millionaires, but obviously they know what they're doing, even if I didn't know what they were doing—at least, not at first. During the experimental stages I felt like Zasu Pitts.

"I've always liked some of the new music, but I noticed a curious thing. A lot of the songs seem to require a vocal group. Can you imagine how much of its effectiveness 'Up, Up And Away' would lose if it were done by a single singer?

"Still, hearing all the great lyrics and music produced by the Beatles, Burt Bacharach, Donovan, Simon and Garfunkel, I knew that we were long past the day when you could combine everything in the same bag and put it down as rock 'n' roll. The only suitable term that takes it all in today is 'contemporary.'

"Working with Koppelman and Rubin changed my whole approach. I was used to hearing demonstration records, talking over material, rehearsing with the rhythm section, selecting my arranger, deciding on a style of interpretation.

"Under the new system, they just sent me lead sheets and I waited for them to call me up. I had nothing to do with the instrumental aspects of the records. When I found out Shorty Rogers was going to arrange and conduct the first session, I felt a lot more secure."

At the session everything fell into place with unexpected ease:

"It wasn't a mechanical process at all.

"They'd put a lot of creative effort into it, preparing backgrounds so that I could just step in and bring my own interpretation of the lyric to whatever they had set up for me."

Above: Peggy Lee flanked by two of her biggest fans—Mel Tormé on her right, and superstar drummer Buddy Rich—at a party honoring Count Basie in September 1974.

key recordings

1942	*"I Got it Bad and That Ain't Good"* with Benny Goodman, taken from the Duke Ellington revue *"Jump For Joy,"* becomes her first hit.
1942	*"Blues in the Night"* with Goodman's sextet.
1942	*"Somebody Else Is Taking My Place"* is Peggy Lee's first No. 1 single.
1942	*"The Way You Look Tonight."*
1943	*"Why Don't You Do Right?"* goes to No. 4.
1945	*"Waitin' for the Train to Come In"*—a Top 10 hit.
1946	*"I Don't Know Enough About You"* also went Top 10.
1947	*"It's a Good Day,"* co-written with husband Dave Barbour, climbs to No. 16.
1947	*"Golden Earrings,"* another Top 10 entry.
1948	*"Mañana,"* co-written with Barbour, who also conducted the orchestra on this No. 1 hit.
1948	*"For Every Man There's a Woman"* marks a reunion with Benny Goodman.
1950	Duet with Mel Tormé, *"The Old Master Painter,"* slides into the Top 10.
1952	*"Lover"* marks a label change to Decca and a search for a new sound.
1952	*"Watermelon Weather,"* duet with Bing Crosby.
1953	*"Black Coffee"* marks her debut as a "serious" album artist.
1955	Peggy featured in the film *Pete Kelly's Blues* with Ella Fitzgerald.
1956	Top 20 hit with *"Mr Wonderful."*
1956	*"Jump for Joy"* LP with arrangements by the legendary Nelson Riddle.
1957	Recorded *"The Man I Love"* LP with Sinatra conducting.
1958	*"Fever"* hits Top 10 charts internationally.
1959	*"Beauty and the Beast"* concert LP with sterling support from sextet led by George Shearing.
1962	*"Sugar and Spice"* and *"Mink Jazz"* recorded with Benny Carter.
1969	Peggy scores Top 40 hit with *"Is That All There Is?"* written by Leiber and Stoller.
1974	*"Let's Love"* LP boasted a title track written and produced by Paul McCartney.
1975	*"Mirrors"* LP features nine Leiber and Stoller songs and a supporting cast of ninety musicians.
1988	*"Peggy Sings the Blues"* marked a return to form.

Anita O'Day, once described as "the greatest white girl jazz singer in the world," was an uncompromising performer who knew exactly what she wanted to hear from her musicians and how to get it. Even when she had a perfect performance "in the can," she would insist on another take to coax that little bit of extra inspiration from her band, and woe betide the soloist who played the same line twice!

Anita was an inspired and authoritative stylist whose logical, rhythmic revisions of the melodic lines were gilded with the subtle inflections and accents of an instrumentalist. And she possessed an astonishing sense of time. For example, she could improvise an exhilarating 10-bar phrase right across the bridge of a track like "Have You Met Miss Jones" in the manner of Stan Getz, while her infallible pitch and intuitive sense of harmony would spot a rogue note, or single out an ingenious harmonic, that only her arrangers could have been expected to identify.

The comparisons with Billie Holiday were perhaps inevitable, particularly on ballads, which she graced with elegance and poise, although on uptempo numbers Anita's playful rephrasing of the melody line and spontaneous scatting helped to establish her in a league of her own. With the possible exception of Lady Day, Anita would brush aside all comparisons with other singers by reminding the presumptuous journalist that she considered herself the very first of her kind —a claim that she had some justification in making.

Born in Chicago on December 18, 1919, Anita began her career while still a teenager, singing for hours on end at the dehumanizing dance marathons that were a product of the Depression. Her first professional engagements came with the Max Miller Combo in 1939, but she went largely unnoticed until she joined Gene Krupa's band two years later and started cutting her first disks, including "Georgia on My Mind."

While the other female singers of the era wore wedding cake dresses and appeared to be content to be decorative additions, Anita sported a band jacket and skirt to show that

she considered herself an integral member of the orchestra. After a spell with Gene Krupa, Anita joined Roy Eldridge and recorded the hits "The Walls Keep Talking" and "Thanks for the Boogie Ride." Then she jumped ship in midstream to join Stan Kenton in 1944. With Kenton she cut what became the bandleader's first national hit, "And Her Tears Flowed Like Wine," but she split after a year to rejoin Krupa, having recommended her replacement, a young singer in the same mold called June Christy. Christy was among the first of a post-war generation of female vocalists to openly base their own style on Anita O'Day, although few could emulate Anita's radical instrumental flair or her sense of swing.

With Krupa, Anita notched up more hits, including "Chickery Chick" and "Opus 1," on which she was inspired to new heights by Sy Oliver's imaginative arrangement.

When she left Krupa for the second time in 1945, it was to pursue a solo career, during which she matured at a remarkable pace. As a freelancer, she received special billing with both Benny Goodman and Duke Ellington, and enjoyed hits as a solo singer including a cover of "Tennessee Waltz."

However, her finest years were still to come under the guidance of the ubiquitous Norman Granz, whom she joined in 1952. Granz teamed her with stellar celebrities such as Oscar Peterson and some of the finest session musicians available, but he also encouraged her to establish her own combo in the belief that a familiar setting would prove more productive than had her habit of flitting between groups. But she remained wilfully, and proudly, independent. And as late as 1993, she was still performing and recording at full tilt with the unsparing energy of a twenty-something. "I look at a song as a horse race," she once remarked, "and I like to finish up out in front."

This interview by Max Jones appeared in the *Melody Maker* dated Christmas Day 1965.

ANITA: RETIRE? I TAKE OUT OCCASIONALLY BUT I NEVER QUIT

You don't have to spend long with Anita O'Day to realize you are with an eager enthusiast of songs and singers—those she likes, at any rate.

"I'm always looking for songs, good songs that I can feel. I want to tell a story when I'm singing, and if I like a song I can really tell it."

I guessed, having heard her sing it, that "Street Of Dreams" was one Anita could feel.

"Right—and isn't that a lovely verse? I like the story and I like the chords. What more could you want? I wish I could find a new song like that I could lay on people. Is anybody writing good songs today?"

"Alec Wilder," I suggested. There was more agreement. "He's done some beautiful things. Do you know a tune he wrote some years ago called 'April Age?' I love that."

At this point, Anita sang the theme softly. Which added a good deal to the atmosphere of the Cumberland Hotel bar in which we were sitting at the time.

"Yes," she said, "I must find Alec Wilder. I really want new songs you know, so will you tell any of your readers who write songs, please send them to Anita, care of the paper."

In the way of singers, Anita's tastes are orthodox insofar as she had endless admiration for Billie Holiday, and puts Ella at number one today.

She spoke very highly of Joe Williams, praised Ernestine Anderson for her natural approach ("Here's what I am") and Ethel Ennis—who is due shortly at Annie's Room—for her intonation ("Her pitching's perfect, which helps").

But she has a special regard for the cool and modern-jazz-influenced singers such as Jackie Cain and Roy Kral, Annie Ross, and Jackie Paris.

"Jackie Paris sings beautifully, plays guitar, he's just great, and he's most underrated. He was already great, and now he's found this girl, Anna-Marie Moss, and they are doing a team thing.

Above: Anita O'Day on stage with the Johnny Dankworth Orchestra at the Marquee Club in London's Oxford Street, in 1961.

Previous Page: Anita photographed in Hollywood in 1955 by William Claxton.

Right: Relaxing before the camera of Herman Leonard during a 1952 Norman Granz recording session in New York.

"They're married, and they work mostly in the East as they live in New York. It's a good duo and would be a good act to bring here."

What is the situation like for jazz singers in the States today?

"Well, in Los Angeles there used to be, say, twelve jazz rooms and these are now down to three. That's about what it's like in general. Nowadays, when I meet friends of mine, they're liable to say: "Where are you blowing now?'

"You have to travel these days to find gigs. I'm here in England; next I go to Hawaii; then I open in Japan. Yes, I think Europe, and England in particular, is going to offer more and more work to jazz musicians. It's fair really, because the jazz clubs in the States were closed by your Beatles."

I wondered if Anita gave the same show here in London as she would do in a club at home. Basically she does, but she explained that her performance depended on the accompanying band.

"You see, I listen to the group I'm working with and take it from there, since I'm an improvising singer. If the piano man I'm with is a distant player, I sing that way. If he's just the regular fifths and sevenths man, then that's the way I sing a song.

"Because I'm not a singer who has a part written out for the band to play 'clink, clink, clink.' I'm not in that kind of a show. If I'm feeling jolly, that's the way it comes out."

Does Anita consider herself to be hard on musicians?

"No, I'm not too exacting. I only hope that a man knows. You can't tell anybody how to play. He has to have the ability to feel how things ought to be played. It's like the old saying: If he has to ask, he'll never know.

"I want musicians to stimulate me, not just follow me. Of course, different groups all have different things. The band at Annie's with me, for instance, is a good swing group. Peter King, who leads the guys, he's excellent. A very competent musician and he improvises well.

"So what I do is the result of the accompaniment. If I find that the players are a bit shallow, musically, I just do it accordingly. Because a mood is a tempo to me, and if it gains momentum it loses the mood for me. I'm sound-conscious you see.

"A big band scene is something else, though. That's what I call pattern work, singing patterns. It's like the band says 'doo wacky doo' and I do 'doo wacky doo.' But in the small group it's open, so I take the lead and then I can take the fills, you know."

People have wondered why Anita O'Day wears a suit for her act when so many singers spread themselves on glittering gowns.

"Why don't I wear gowns? I can wear them, and I do for certain work. But I started wearing suits years ago, and I always go back to it. I wear a suit like the band.

"I find it relaxes me, and what good is a nervous singer? Especially when she's trying to think, which I do when I'm singing."

Where are future girl jazz singers to come from?

"That's it! Where? Where are they going to get the experience now there are no big bands to work with. First, a girl's got to find out what she can do, then where she can do it."

Does Anita ever think of retiring?

"You mean, what keeps me singing? I couldn't quit. Like I told you earlier, this is my mission. I take out occasionally but I never quit. And I just kind of hope it continues. I'll tell you, I love to find people who dig the same kind of music I like"

Above: Deep in discussion with drum star and early mentor Gene Krupa (note the sticks in his back pocket) during the 1952 Granz recording date.

Above right: The same session, with arranger Quincy Jones and trumpet maestro Roy Eldridge, the latter with whom Anita had worked many times over the years.

key recordings

1941-3 Her first recordings cut with drummer Gene Krupa and his band including *"Just a Little Bit South of North Carolina"* and *"Georgia on My Mind."*

1941-3 Anita records duets with Roy Eldridge (*"Let Me Off Uptown"*) and singer Johnny Desmond (*"Two in Love"*), who was known as "the GI Sinatra."

1941-56 Anita appears in a series of short promo films with Kenton and Krupa.

1944 First hit with Stan Kenton, *"And Her Tears Flowed Like Wine."*

1945 Back with Gene Krupa she recorded *"Boogie Blues,"* *"Chickery Chick,"* and *"Opus 1."*

1947 Top 30 hit *"Hi Ho Trailus Boot Whip"* as featured vocalist with Alvy West and the Little Band. This and other recordings with the Little Band were later issued on the CD *"I Told Ya I Love You, Now Get Out."*

1951 Solo success came with a cover of the Patti Page song *"Tennessee Waltz"* on the London label.

1952 The first of her albums for Norman Granz's Verve label, *"Sings Jazz,"* recorded with the Roy Kral Combo.

1954 *"Songs by Anita O'Day"* recorded with her own combo.

1955 Albums *"Anita"* and *"Pick Yourself Up"* recorded with Buddy Bregman.

1956 Anita rejoins Gene Krupa and Roy Eldridge to celebrate old times on the album *"Drummer Man."*

1957 *"Sings for Oscar"* unites Anita with Oscar Peterson. It was reissued as *"Anita Sings the Most."*

1958 Release of *"At Mr. Kelly's"* and *"Sings the Winners"* recorded with the Russ Garcia and Marty Paich bands.

1959 *"Cool Heat"* with multi-reed player Jimmy Giuffre.

1959 Anita collaborates with Billy May for the LP *"Swings Cole Porter"* and again the following year for *"Anita O'Day and Billy May Swing Rodgers and Hart."*

1959 Anita plays herself in the movie *The Gene Krupa Story*.

1960 *"Incomparable!"* with Bill Holman.

1960 Anita teams up with Russ Garcia once more for *"Waiter Make Mine Blues."*

1960 Film of her set at the 1958 Newport Jazz Festival released to cinemas as *Jazz on a Summer's Day*.

1970 *"In Berlin"* on her own AOD label captured her in performance at the Berlin Festival.

1975-8 To capitalize on a series of highly successful tours of Japan, Anita releases six albums, including *"Live In Tokyo,"* *"My Ship,"* *"Live at Mingos,"* and *"Angel Eyes,"* which were later released on her own Emily label.

1978-9 Debut of her septet featuring Lou Levy on the album *"There's Only One,"* followed by *"Mello' Day."*

1985 *"S' Wonderful"* LP with Hank Jones' big band.

1991 Still going strong at age 71, Anita releases *"At Vine Street Live."*

1993 *"Rules of the Road"* LP with singer Jack Sheldon's big band.

When the ebullient British jazz singer Annie Ross recorded Stephen Sondheim's "Some People," about the joys of living life to the full, she might have been singing about her own eclectic career. Not content to be remembered as part of the innovative, Grammy-award-winning vocalese trio Lambert, Hendricks, and Ross, she bounced back from early retirement to run a prestigious jazz club in London during the early 60s, and then went on to establish a solo stage and screen career that would have been the envy of any serious actress.

Annie was born Annabelle Short in the leafy suburbs of Mitcham, Surrey, on July 25, 1930. Her parents were Scottish show business pros who brought their daughter up north of the border, where she acquired the strong brogue that was to give her singing voice a distinctive edge.

When she was four she was sent to live with her aunt, the Broadway star Ella Logan, in Los Angeles. It was Ella who guided Annie's first steps in show business, securing her a spot on a Paul Whiteman radio talent show, which she won, and a speaking part in an "Our Gang" film at the age of five.

At the age of 13, Annie had progressed to playing Judy Garland's sister in "Presenting Lily Mars," but four years later she turned her back on a promising movie career to live in Paris, where she sang with jazz émigrés such as Coleman Hawkins and touring outfits including the Lionel Hampton big band.

On her return to America her punishing self-imposed schedule saw her subbing for Billie Holiday at the Apollo—and winning over that notoriously unforgiving audience—then flying between London and New York to appear in revue with Anthony Newley.

When the opportunity came for Annie to make her first records, she rejected the easier option of reworking straight cover versions and, instead, being a precocious talent with burning ambition, opted for a demanding vocalese style (putting words to established instrumental tunes), which had only been attempted sporadically by singers Marion Harris, Eddie Jefferson, and King Pleasure.

Her first excursion in this idiom was the 1952 single "Twisted," based on a tenor solo by Wardell Gray. Annie's lyrics, which offered a distinctly oblique view of psychoanalysis, introduced a streak of black humor to jazz, which was to set her songs apart from the mainstream. But even more than her wit and verbal agility, it was her vocal dexterity that persuaded singer-songwriter Jon Hendricks and his partner Dave Lambert to ask Annie to participate in a unique and challenging project.

She was brought in to coach a mass chorus of voices to sing the instrumental parts for a Count Basie tribute album, but the chorus couldn't swing. And so Annie found herself dubbing all the parts with Hendricks and Lambert, accompanied by a small ensemble. It was the beginning of a distinguished musical partnership, which saw the trio regularly break attendance records in clubs across America, and produce a clutch of first class albums before Annie was forced to retire five years later from exhaustion.

Hendrix and Lambert replaced her with Yolande Bavan, but called it a day when Bavan quit two years later. Annie, meanwhile, recovered sufficiently to sustain a solo career back home in Britain during the early 60s and run her jazz club, Annie's Room, in Covent Garden.

In the 1970s, she gravitated back to stage and screen, starring in *The Threepenny Opera* with Vanessa Redgrave, Weill and Brecht's *The Seven Deadly Sins* for the Royal Ballet, and a Royal Festival Hall concert celebrating the music of Kurt Weill under the baton of André Previn.

Her screen credits include the Hammer schlock horror classic *Straight on Till Morning* (for which she also provided the theme song), *Superman 3*, *Throw Mama off the Train*, two films with Robert Altman, *Short Cuts* and *The Player*, a couple of kitsch cult horror flicks, and *Send in the Girls*, a small-screen TV series about the music business. And in 1992 she proved her humor and voice still had an edge, appearing as an aging singer in an episode of the TV series *WKRP In Cincinnati,* appropriately titled *Mama Was A Rolling Stone*.

A *Melody Maker* article sensationally sub-headed "Annie Ross blows the lid off the jazz world," heralded Ross' final break with the Lambert, Hendricks, and Ross trio in 1962, in an exclusive interview which described—in candid detail by the standards of the music journalism of the day—some of the personal problems that contributed to her departure.

I WAS ONE BIG HELL OF A . . . WRECK !

The last has almost certainly been heard of the great modernist vocal threesome Lambert, Hendricks, and Ross.

For 31-year-old Scots-born (sic) Annie Ross is recovering from a complete nervous collapse, and has doubts of ever returning to the States as a jazz singer.

The boys are back in America with Ceylon-born Yolande Bavan as Annie's stand-in.

She may well become Annie's replacement.

Annie is at present living with her brother, the well-known Scots comedian Jimmy Logan, in the country home of the Marchioness of Graham in Stirlingshire.

SOMETHING NEW

"And I've got to thinking that now ought to be the time for me to go out on my own and broaden my scope a lot," she told the *Melody Maker* in an exclusive interview.

"Fans may think that there is tremendous excitement being a singer who is always looking for something new in technique.

"But frankly it gets more than just a bit frustrating always being so way out of your audiences that only a fraction of them understand or appreciate what you are doing."

Above: Recording an album of songs by the poet Christopher Logue, with music by British drummer Tony Kinsey and Stanley Myers; London, 1963.

Previous page: Annie with Dave Lambert (left) and Jon Hendricks.

Below: Backstage at the Trocadero in London's Elephant and Castle district, 1962. Picture by Val Wilmer, one of Britain's leading music photographers.

Above: A glamorously clad Annie appearing at the Berlin Jazz Festival in July 1970.

COMMERCIAL

"I've given it all a great deal of thought recently. There has been plenty of time for thinking these last few weeks.

"I'm pretty sure now that I'd prefer to broaden my scope, do more commercial songs in the future.

"Don't get me wrong—I'm not thinking of going entirely square.

"But I can't stand people who insist that if you like modern jazz you can't like anything else.

"As long as it's good I like it.

"And there is a lot of music I'd like to sing that's just not perhaps the swingiest of stuff but is, for my money, easy on the ear and satisfying to the singer.

"I realize that I have a certain loyalty to the boys. We've been through a lot together.

"But I owe a lot to myself, too.

"Jazz singing in the States is the most awful soul-destroying rat race on earth," she went on.

"It's nothing but a grinding succession of one night stands, traveling and recording.

"The last things you get time for are sleep or decent feeding.

"You get so wound up on the merry-go-round you don't even know what time it is. With me work became so that to be without it left me edgy and sort of empty.

"You get so excited with the whirl, with the successes, and the sheer swing of life that you don't realize that you are living a ghastly, abnormal existence that can only ruin you in the end.

"You go from smoky club to smoky club without realizing that even the most enthusiastic jazz lover must have a break from the sound of it, the smell and the weight of it.

TREATMENT

"Having had this breakdown and this divorce from that life, I frankly don't look forward to going back to that sort of life.

"I keep putting the day of going back further and further from my mind. All I want to do now is rest and get well.

"For the first time in months I feel relaxed. There isn't anything sitting on my head any more."

Annie was ordered into a nursing home by her doctor immediately after she returned from the Continental tour with the boys and the Basie band show.

"I was all shot to pieces and a great big hell of a wreck," she admitted in the interview.

"The doctor warned me that if I didn't submit to the proper treatment and rest, then he couldn't be held responsible for what might happen to me later."

While she was in the clinic her brother, Jimmy Logan, arranged to rent the Graham house as a convalescence for Annie.

NURSING HOME

"I talked it over with Jon and Dave before I went into the nursing home. They realized it was going to be the best for all of us in the long run. They assured me that when I'm ready to go back they'll be ready to receive me.

"But . . ." and she paused heavily for a few moments. ". . . oh, I don't know if I'll ever go back really."

Nina Simone is an artist of intense commitment and apparent contradictions. For one, she is a superb intuitive jazz singer and a classically trained pianist who delights in embracing a diverse range of styles, including gospel, blues, showbiz standards, and pop. She takes a particular pride in being worshiped as the "High Priestess of Soul," but readily admits that soul is a quality that she finds notoriously hard to define. She is also a fine songwriter who has penned hits for other artists, while she herself has only charted with cover versions. In particular, her interpretations of Kurt Weill should be singled out for contrasting a smouldering intensity with an almost fatalistic nonchalance, to which the composer would surely have given his approval.

Perhaps a clue to the enigma is to be found in her definition of jazz as meaning "freedom," including the freedom to defy categorization. Certainly, Simone has done much to broaden that definition both in her musical career and in her campaigns as a self-professed black activist in the cause of racial tolerance.

Nina was born Eunice Waymon on February 21, 1933, in Tryon, North Carolina, to parents who were both Methodist clergy. She was one of eight musically gifted children, but apparently distinguished herself by playing the piano by ear at the age of three. By eight she had enrolled in the prestigious Juilliard School of Music in New York, where she discovered her own vocal ability by accompanying other singers.

She began singing professionally in 1954 under her adopted stage name, which she took in tribute to the French film actress Simone Signoret. It had not been her intention to pursue a singing career, but she changed her mind after being booked into a nightclub in Atlantic City as a pianist and seeing the distress of the owner, who had been told to expect a singer! Her eclectic repertoire soon drew a wide audience, among whom were talent scouts from the King label. Being R&B specialists, King didn't know quite how to handle her, and so sidelined her to their jazz subsidiary, Bethlehem.

Billie Holiday had been an early influence from whom Nina acquired an affection for jazz with a blues tint. From Billie she also developed a fondness for the Gershwin song "I Loves You Porgy," which was to be her first chart hit for King in 1959. But while Nina went on to become a influential figure in the early 60s, with recordings of songs that others were to make hits (namely "Don't Let Me Be Misunderstood," "I Put a Spell on You," and her own song "To Be Young, Gifted, and Black"), her ambivalent image and uncompromising attitude to the music business meant that she remained a concert, club, and festival favorite rather than a regular visitor to the charts.

She did not have another hit until 1968, when her version of "Ain't Got No – I Got Life," from the rock musical *Hair* lodged near the top of the charts, to be followed by "To Love Somebody," which The Bee Gees had written with the late Otis Redding in mind.

In the 1970s, Nina continued to play to packed houses on the cabaret and club circuit, but was dedicating more of her time and effort into her role as a spokesperson for the Civil Rights movement. Her political activities and her politically provocative statements in songs such as "Mississippi Goddamn" alienated a section of her audience, and gave several record company executives a migraine or two.

In a career spanning 50 years, she recorded for more than a dozen different record labels, including several small independent companies in France, where she found a loyal following. But although Nina might have professed an indifference to commercial success, she achieved it again anyway when her 1959 recording of "My Baby Just Cares For Me'" was used in a TV advertisement for Chanel perfume. The single was swiftly reissued and hit the Top 10 in charts all over Europe, followed by a slew of retrospective compilations, all of which sold well and introduced her to an entirely new audience.

An interview by Michael Smith, which appeared on December 7, 1968, focused on Nina Simone's uncompromising views about race attitudes, racial equality, and her own reputation as a "difficult" performer to deal with.

THE OTHER (MORE SERIOUS) SIDE OF NINA . . .

At the Montreux Jazz Festival this year, the Casino was so packed for a concert by Nina Simone that many people, myself among them, were obliged to watch her performance on closed circuit television.

Filtration through electronic circuits inevitably diminishes any performance, particularly in the case of so superbly endowed a stage artist as Nina Simone, now captivating the British public with her hit "I Ain't Go No – I Got Life."

But a major compensating factor on this occasion was the fact that I was watching the box in the company of Kenny Clarke, Art Taylor, Jack de Johnette, and Benny Bailey.

And if I had ever had any doubt that Nina Simone, the high priestess of soul, knows how to "tell it like it is," then a glance at the faces of these musicians provided abundant reassurance.

Musicians are not easily spellbound—but these four were completely captivated, and you could feel their common pride as they watched Nina Simone take what was a predominantly white (and initially indifferent) audience, and by sheer artistry, by strength of character, and magical judgment, drive them into what can only be described as a mood of ecstatic acclamation. This was Black Power in its most dignified and enriching sense.

And as she had them on their feet, begging for more, the outbreak of grins and nudges on my left made me feel indecently white.

Nina Simone not only communicates, but she can create in an audience the need to receive and exalt in that communication. "Now, listen," she says severely . . . and, like admonished children, the audience listens with rapt intensity.

Right: Photographed by David Redfern in 1984, Nina performing at London's leading jazz venue, Ronnie Scott's.

She has been known to get fairly tough with audiences in the past, and at Antibes on one occasion she abandoned the lyric of a song and substituted a spontaneous chorus, in which she roundly cussed her musicians for not keeping time.

If you ask Nina whether it is true that she is difficult to work with, she says, disarmingly, "Yes. I demand of my musicians what I demand of myself. I set very high standards because I'm a musician myself. Maybe, just once in a while, I might really please myself, but more often, I don't. There is always something you could have done better."

She says she doesn't lose her temper with an audience too often these days. "It's a long time since I 'blessed' out an audience—and when I did they didn't really understand what I was saying half the time. I try to adapt to the mood of an audience—try to get them involved. I like to think they know what I'm trying to communicate and that when I leave an audience, I've made some contact with them.

"But all art has the same laws of discipline. You learn your craft well, but you are rarely completely satisfied with it. Great painters, for example, are hardly ever pleased with their work."

She loves playing to European audiences and admits that some of the appreciation she gets from Europe is bound up with her association with the Civil Rights movement.

"But people in Europe are so well informed. They seem to know all my records and when they were made.

"I suppose the Civil Rights thing does come into it, and has some bearing on their response, but in a lot of cases I'm sure it has nothing to do with it."

Nina Simone doesn't operate in any one specific idiom of popular music, and says, "I'd like to be remembered and known as a performer who plays and sings. I don't really fit into any category and it is as difficult for me to describe myself as it is for writers to describe me."

SOUL

"I've been called the High Priestess of Soul—and I like that. But I just haven't got the words to describe what I do. It's like love. How do you talk about love?

"Soul is hard to define. Words don't begin to describe the feelings many people have about so many things—words are so inadequate. Soul, of course, is particularly associated with Negroes, but it's not just music—it goes much broader and deeper."

Miss Simone said she wouldn't care to name any white musicians who had soul—"but it's not the same kind we got. It was Negro music first and, if that is the basic premise, then white musicians are trying to get the same feeling—and they can, up to a point. But we are the originators and we should be the critics.

"Soul includes a man's background, the way he lives, his language, his work—and if you talk about it in that way, then, of course, a white artist can have soul."

As a proud champion of her race, it is inevitable that Nina Simone is involved in the racial issue, but she says quite firmly, "I can't stand politics. I'm not a politician. But when I'm on stage, of course I'm conscious that I'm colored."

SOCIAL

"I feel that I am upholding the prestige of my people and most of my songs are about the problem. But I never forget that my first purpose is to bring art to the people; any social feeling I have must not overwhelm

109

Below: Nina Simone making an appearance at the Newport Jazz Festival in 1967.

my music or be taken to extremes." Not that Nina Simone has not felt driven to extreme measures on occasions.

After the Mississippi riots happened, she asked her husband, Andy Stroud, to teach her how to handle a zip gun. And she says: "I'm not beyond killing—nobody is. But," and she smiled broadly, "I wrote 'Mississippi Goddamn' instead."

She feels that the Civil Rights situation is getting better in some ways and worse in others, and said: "In the book *Sippi* by John Killens it says that when the Supreme Court upheld the Civil Rights issue in 1964, most Negroes thought Jim Crow had been buried.

'Yet now there is even more ill feeling than before. Everybody thought it was a good decision, and nobody knows why it brought violence. It meant a radical change in the attitude of the Negro, regardless of age or political affiliation. And this book has to do with the attitudes of people since the Supreme Court decision.

"Maybe paying lip service to equality is one thing, and living it is entirely another. The violence is going to get much worse. But the Negro revolution is only one aspect of increasing violence and unrest in the world. The whole world is turning upside down. It is the age of Aquarius —white and black."

Below: It's Nina at Newport again, this time in 1968.

110

As a celebrated and successful artist, Nina Simone is somewhat protected from the more vicious manifestations of racial prejudice but, she says, she can sense its presence in many places. And, when you are on the receiving end, there really isn't all that much to choose between a police fascist's truncheon and the disdainful sniff of a "superior" white.

"I've found prejudice in Britain, in Holland, and even in Morocco. In Morocco I encountered some English people in a hotel who showed their prejudice—so we got up and walked out.

"Now, I love being in London—it has its own personality and character, and I love the way the people talk; but I don't really feel any more welcome in London than I do at home."

THEMES

Nina Simone is certain that the color problem will get very much worse before it gets better, and she fears there will be a great deal of violence and bloodshed before "Mississippi Goddamn" becomes an outdated theme.

Like all the songs she writes, that one "just happened because I was inspired. The songs just come—I don't work at it." Spontaneity and naturalness are two of Nina Simone's most shining virtues, but she has her talents in other fields than stage performances and recording.

"I would love to sing the themes to some movies and do at least one movie as an actress—just to see what it's like."

In the course of her recording career, Nina has made two dozen albums, and says she likes about five of them, "one of these being 'Pastel Blues,' which I made around 1965."

When she's relaxing she likes to listen to records, the type of music varying according to the mood she's in. "If I'm in a swinging mood, I like to play music I can dance to. In a relaxed mood I like to play Bach. I also love to listen to Ray Charles, Aretha Franklin, and Betty Carter—I admire her singing tremendously and I try to see her whenever I can.

"In the jazz field, Coltrane and Monk are the two who stand out the most as far as I am concerned."

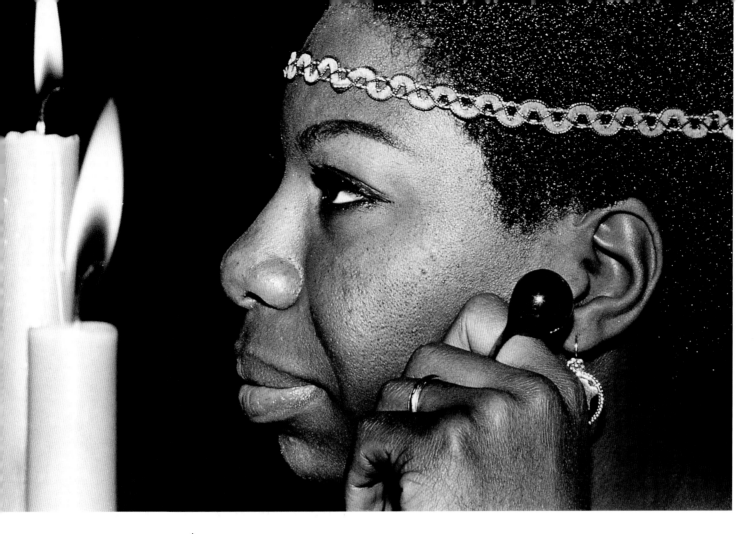

Above: A close-up of Nina by Dezo Hoffman, a music photographer best known for his work with British pop stars, most famously the Beatles.

key recordings

1957   Nina records versions of *"Don't Smoke in Bed"* and *"Plain Gold Ring,"* which later inspire kd lang and Nick Cave to record these songs in the same style.

1959   First single *"I Loves You Porgy"* charts at No. 18 in the pop chart and No. 2 in the R&B chart; it is followed by the singles *"Little Girl Blue"* and *"For All We Know."*

1960   *"Wild Is the Wind"* LP recorded with a trio for Colpix; other highlights of *"The Colpix Years"* included versions of *"Forbidden Fruit," "Gin House Blues,"* and an album of Duke Ellington tunes (1962).

1961   *"Nina at Newport"* live LP makes US Top 30.

1964   *"In Concert"* album (which includes the controversial *"Mississippi Goddamn"*) recorded in New York.

1965   *"I Put a Spell on You"* LP (later combined on CD with *"In Concert"*).

1966-74 A relatively lengthy spell under contract for RCA produces the albums *"Here Comes the Sun," "Sings the Blues,"* and *"Sings Billie Holiday."*

1966   The title track to the *"Please Don't Let Me Be Misunderstood"* album was picked up by UK producer Mickie Most and made into a hit for R&B group The Animals.

1967   LP *"Highpriestess of Soul"* named after the nickname she was given by other musicians.

1968   Live album *"Nuff Said!"* recorded the night after the assassination of Martin Luther King and heavily edited to tone down her political statements. On reissue the cuts were restored.

1968   No, 2 hit with *"Ain't Got No – I Got Life,"* a song from the musical *Hair*. Nina had recorded an orchestral version for the single but her label chose the small ensemble version from her current album.

1968   Another hit earned for a cover of the Gibb brothers' *"To Love Somebody."*

1969   Self-penned *"To Be Young, Gifted, and Black"* is a Top 100 entry, while the reggae-styled cover by Bob and Maria becomes a Top 10 single; the song was also covered by Aretha Franklin in 1972.

1969   Nina releases a version of the Beatles' *"Revolution"* on single.

1969   *"A Very Rare Evening with Nina Simone"* LP.

1978   A soft rock collection, *"Baltimore,"* took its title from the opening track written by Randy Newman.

1981   Nina re-records *"I Loves You Porgy"* for the Salsoul label.

1982   *"Fodder on My Wings"* was a partly French language concept album on the theme of her renunciation of the USA.

1987   *"Live at Ronnie Scott's"* seemed to herald a return to form, but she failed to appear for a return visit amid rumors of personal problems and increasing unreliability.

1987   *"My Baby Just Cares for Me"* used in a Chanel TV ad sells 175,000 copies in the first week on reissue; it eventually hits No. 5 in the British singles chart.

1988-9 Compilation *"The Nina Simone Collection"* followed by *"The Nina Simone Story."*

frank   sinatra   113

Bing Crosby once famously remarked, "Frank Sinatra is the kind of singer who comes along once in a lifetime —but why did it have to be my lifetime?" Such was the size of the shadow cast by the man they called "The Voice."

Other epithets for Francis Albert Sinatra (born Frank Sinestro on December 12, 1915, in Hoboken, New Jersey) included "The Sultan of Swoon," which was a reference to the scenes of near hysteria that he generated among the bobbysoxers in the early 1940s, in a foretaste of the pop phenomena.

With an unrivaled record of chart success, Sinatra was arguably the most popular singer of the 20th century, racking up 156 hit singles, including 33 in the Top 10 between 1943 and 1975, and 50 hit albums between 1946 and 1981, including 13 in the Top 5. It was probably his unprecedented popularity rather than his smooth singing style that prevented the jazz purists from acknowledging his talent, and yet he was a supreme and intuitive stylist in the jazz idiom whenever he found the company congenial and the setting to his taste. His material may have crossed the tracks into the mainstream, but Frank's flawless phrasing, intonation, and sense of rhythm demonstrated a jazz sensibility and an instinctive sense of swing.

While reports of his notoriously short temper, stormy private life, and alleged gangland connections suggested that he could be a difficult man to work with, and perhaps even impossible to live with, when it came to performing he was a perfectionist who never allowed his personality or ego to dominate a song. He would seduce a ballad as he would a classy dame, waltzing it around a little, familiarizing himself with its subtle and capricious changes of mood, before turning on the charm. A tender but firm embrace and it would surrender, both singer and song becoming as inseparable as lovers. An uptempo tune would get the more direct approach, although there would always be the pretense of detachment as Frank affected a casual, off-hand manner. But the surface sheen hid a singular sensitivity. When the magic was working at this unique intensity, few could resist falling under the spell.

Yet his inimitable technique was not there from the outset. It had to be nurtured to maturity. Frank first attracted attention as a featured vocalist with the Harry James Orchestra in 1939, with which he made his first (uncredited) recording, "All or Nothing at All." It sold a disappointing 8000 copies when first released, but was to be a No. 1 when it was reissued in 1943.

On the recommendation of a CBS radio executive, he joined Tommy Dorsey in 1940 and within a year he had knocked Crosby from the top slot in the influential *Downbeat* poll, although he remained uncredited on the Dorsey recordings, several of which hit the top spot. In one of his rare candid moments, Sinatra acknowledged his debt to Dorsey for teaching him the importance of breath control and phrasing in the manner of the great instrumentalists, although he must have been frustrated about the fact that he had been denied a credit on the records, for in 1943 he left to pursue a solo career. That same year he also made the first of nearly 50 variable movies that helped to redefine him as an all-round entertainer, and were to include the musicals *On the Town*, *Guys and Dolls,* and *High Society*.

With conductor and arranger Axel Stordahl, Sinatra made the first of 86 hit singles for Columbia, including "You'll Never Know" and "Saturday Night Is the Loneliest Night of the Week," then trumped them with what is acknowledged to be the first concept album in history, "The Voice" (a No. 1 LP in 1946).

His greatest recordings, however, are without doubt the dozen albums he made with Nelson Riddle between 1954 and 1961, which, together with his Oscar winning performance in the war movie *From Here to Eternity*, revived his career after a hiatus in the late 1940s and early 50s. Riddle's jazz-tinged arrangements on classic albums such as "In the Wee Small Hours" (1955), and "Songs for Swinging Lovers" (1956), treated the voice as a solo instrument, to be answered by muted trumpet or underscored by strings rather than accompanied by the orchestra, as many jazz vocalists would demand. It was a stroke of genius, providing a repertoire of standards he would mine for the rest of his 60-year career.

When he left Capitol to set up his own Reprise label in 1961, he continued to mint sparkling singles such as the surprise No. 1 "Strangers in the Night" (1966) and the number that became his theme song. "My Way" (1969).

Right: Arranger Axel Stordahl with his back to the camera while Frank studies the lyrics.

On October 18, 1953, *Melody Maker* ran a major piece subtitled "Frank Sinatra, one of the world's outstanding entertainers, writes his personal opinions on one of the world's toughest problems."

FRANK SINATRA SAYS—JAZZ HAS NO COLOR BAR!

I've been up and down America a lot since I first started singing and I've seen and heard a lot to make me feel both proud and ashamed of being an American. I've seen racial and religious intolerance take all kind of forms, and many times I've seen one man's hand raised against his brother simply because he didn't like the color of his skin.

I have also seen decency and sanity rise out of the depths of depression and fear, and assert themselves in truly wonderful ways.

It is not my task to preach to anyone or sell social messages to my fellow citizens, but I happen to hold a few firm convictions about life and about democracy.

I hold certain definite opinions about some of the problems currently dividing our nation and frequently I feel the urge to express myself, to speak out on issues that entertainers don't normally concern themselves with.

I believe that an entertainer's function is to entertain.

But one is also a responsible citizen with all the same rights and obligations as the next man.

When an entertainer shirks his duty as a citizen in a crisis, he is as much to be criticized as anybody else. And when he faces up courageously to an issue which, because of its national importance, affects him directly, he is entitled to applause.

Louis Armstrong, who I've long admired for his artistry, faced up to a great national issue last September and sounded off strongly in an interview given to a newspaperman in Grand Forks, North Dakota.

ANGRY

Louis was understandably angry over the failure of the federal government to act quickly and firmly to protect the right of nine Negro students to go to a high school in Little Rock without being segregated.

A lot of people sided with Armstrong on that deal. Others said he was too outspoken and should not make statements outside the area of music.

Though I felt at the time that Pops might have left out a few of those harsh words about his president and government, I believe he was basically right and perfectly justified in saying what he did.

Left: Sinatra running through some song arrangements in 1960 with dancers in the background awaiting their call.

His was a righteous indignation over injustice.

When Nat King Cole was assaulted on a theater stage by bigoted hoodlums in Birmingham, Alabama, the whole of the entertainment profession experienced a sense of outrage.

I was furious when I heard of the incident and immediately tried to reach Nat by phone to see how he was feeling and to tell him of my own personal anger at what had happened.

I finally reached him in a motel on the road at 3 am the following morning, and conveyed my concern and sympathy, and I simply said I was shocked, sorry, and angry over the outrage.

CLASSY

Nat is not only a great entertainer but a first-rate citizen, a very classy gentleman who honors his profession wherever he appears. I am proud to count him as a friend.

I have a lot of friends in show business and they come from all walks of life and represent almost every imaginable skin tint.

Friendship to me results from a warm and lasting meeting of minds and hearts and cannot possibly be based on such irrelevant factors as color, class, or creed.

Sammy Davis, Jr., is one of the world's most gifted entertainers and one of the most successful. I've known him since he was a child performer traveling the vaudeville and club circuit with his uncle and father and living out of trunks.

My affection for him reaches beyond his great talent and touches certain human qualities that would move me regardless of who it was that possessed them.

To me he represents the finest traditions in our business. His talents are so staggering that each time I see him I experience a greater thrill.

I have said I wouldn't follow this man into any club or theater anywhere, not for all the gold in Las Vegas. I am proud of his fabulous success which he has earned the hard way and fully deserves.

Professionally and musically, I can't begin to fully evaluate the tremendous importance of Negro singers and musicians to my development as a singer. The debt I owe them is too immense ever to be repaid.

It has been much more than a long association. I have been on the receiving end of inspiration from a succession of great Negro singers and jazz artists stretching all the way back to early Louis Armstrong and Duke Ellington, who is happily at last being recognized as one of his country's most distinguished composers.

In terms of my singing I have sometimes been asked how it all began, and it's usually been a little hard for me to set the story down in any continuous narrative.

From the days of my childhood I've been listening to sounds and singers, both colored and white, and absorbing a little bit here and a little bit there.

Left: Frank in rehearsal for a tour of Britain in the summer of 1953— the newspaper story that ran underneath was headlined "He Keeps On Crooning."

Countless musicians of talent have helped. But it is Billie Holiday, who I first heard in 52nd Street clubs in the early 1930s, who was, and still remains, the greatest single musical influence on me.

HOLIDAY

It has been a warm and wonderful influence, and I am very proud to acknowledge it. Lady Day is unquestionably the most important influence on American popular singing in the last 20 years.

With a few exceptions, every major pop singer in the US during her generation has been touched in some way by her genius.

The depth of Lady's singing has always rocked me. When I first heard her, standing under a spotlight in a 52nd Street jazz spot, swaying with the beat, I was dazzled by her soft, breathtaking beauty. It was the kind of face that made a man want to touch it tenderly.

When I was a youngster struggling to find myself, I heard a lot of Ethel Waters, whose feeling for the blues and great warmth touched me deep down. I shall never forget her.

The art of Ella Fitzgerald has grown beautifully with the years and it has carried me right along with it. She is, in my opinion, the greatest of all contemporary jazz singers.

There were many other great Negro jazzmen who I met along the way and whose art helped to educate me musically. Listing them all would be a mighty undertaking, but Lester Young, Ben Webster, the late Sid Catlett, Roy Eldridge, Charlie Shavers, Harry Edison, Johnny Hodges, the late Art Tatum, Earl Hines, Teddy Wilson, and Count Basie figure prominently in it.

Of today's younger musicians, Buddy Collette, Chico Hamilton, Miles Davis, and Max Roach are among my special favorites.

My experiences in music have taught me that talent has a blindness to color. Jazz has become an international force simply because the skills and creative talents of musicians of many colors and nations have combined to make it what it is.

America is a great blending of peoples of all shades and beliefs. This blending of the human race has been going on since the beginning of time, and nothing can stop it at this late period.

It really is the most natural thing in life. I get disgusted when I hear bigots denouncing integration in the schools because, if it is charged, it will lead to race-mixing.

TRAGIC

In my own profession, show business, we have always felt proud of our tradition that performers should be rated and accepted on merit and nothing else.

Entertainment on the whole has generally been ahead of the rest of the country in the matter of equal treatment and real democracy.

There remain a few areas where a lot of work has to be done. For instance, in music it's still a tragic fact that a number of cities still have segregated locals of the musicians' union. That, too, will pass.

Recording and radio studios are becoming increasingly integrated.

When I do a recording session for Capitol Records the orchestra backing me up is picked for musical standards alone, and the result is that men like Harry Edison and Buddy Collette are invariably included and playing behind me.

Some people have wanted to know why I am so interested in such things as discrimination and prejudice.

I've been opposed to bigotry all my life because it's wrong and indecent and because the people who practice it are hurting the country and making life miserable for others.

In my own experience I've known prejudice of another sort. A lot of people look down on Italians. Not long ago, a woman, slightly drunk, sat at my table in a night club near Carmel, California, and told me:

"You know what we call you in our house?—the wop singer."

That wasn't the first time I've been called "wop" and it probably won't be the last. But I intend to go on doing what I can to eliminate this kind of sickness.

. The hope for a happy and better future and improved race relations will lie ultimately with the young people of this country.

HOPEFUL

By and large, I think we can depend on them to do a good job in building the kind of democracy we want, respected all over the world.

I repeat, I am hopeful that these problems can and will be licked. The most important thing is to bring people of all kinds together, to establish healthy contact between them.

Once that is done, fear and distrust will vanish and people will stop looking at each other as members of minorities and begin to regard and accept them as human beings.

118

Below: Frank Sinatra in the 1940s, recording the Johnny Mercer classic "Laura," with his long-time collaborator and arranger Axel Stordahl; the two first worked together when Stordahl was arranger with the legendary Tommy Dorsey band.

Above: Dubbed the "musician's singer," Frank Sinatra had an instinctive feel and understanding of the technicalities of the music-making process. As always in command, here in the early 1960s "Ol' Blue Eyes" puts the studio orchestra through their paces during a Reprise recording session.

key recordings

1939 Recording debut (July 13)—uncredited vocalist on *"From the Bottom of My Heart"* by Harry James and his orchestra.

1940 First hit—as featured vocalist on Tommy Dorsey and his orchestra's *"Polka Dots and Moonbeams."* Also sang on the band's *"I'll Never Smile Again"*—which topped the first official US chart.

1942 *"Night and Day"* was his first solo US hit.

1943 The bobbysoxers' idol had his first million seller, *"All or Nothing at All"*—a re-release of a 1939 recording with Harry James' orchestra.

1946 *"Five Minutes More"* became his first solo US No. 1.

1954 After his Oscar-winning performance in *From Here to Eternity* (1953) and a label change to Capitol, Sinatra had major international hits with *"Young at Heart"* and *"Three Coins in the Fountain"* (his first UK No. 1).

1956 The 1950s' biggest-selling album artist released *Songs for Swinging Lovers* LP—the first LP to sell enough to enter the UK singles chart.

1958 Both *"Frank Sinatra Sings Only for the Lonely"* and the Grammy-winning *"Come Fly with Me"* headed the US LP chart.

1961 Launched his own label Reprise —his first LP, *"Ring-A-Ding Ding!"* reached the Top 10.

1966 *"Strangers in the Night"* became his first transatlantic No. 1.

1967 Duet with daughter Nancy, *"Somethin' Stupid,"* topped the transatlantic charts.

1969 Theme song, *"My Way,"* released—it spent a record 124 weeks on the UK chart.

1977 26th UK Top 10 album, *"Portrait of Sinatra,"* becomes his first No. 1.

1986 Six-year-old single, *"Theme from New York, New York"* returned him to UK Top 10.

1993 The album *"Duets,"* on which he sings with many current stars, reached runner-up position in America and sold over 5 million globally. A single from it, *"I've Got You Under My Skin"* (with Bono from U2) reached UK Top 10.

1994 *"Duets II"* reached the US Top 10. It was his 33rd Top 10 entry—a total no other solo performer can match.

1997 An album, *"My Way – The Best Of,"* reached the UK Top 20 —it was still on the chart the day he died.

Mel Tormé, the "singer's singer," as he was often called, was a musician who had fully mastered his instrument. The "velvet fog" that enriched his early pre-LP-era recordings had lifted by his early 30 to reveal a purer, warmer, and more expressive tone, which was the envy of his contemporaries and the delight of his fans.

Mel's 1956 recording of "Mountain Greenery" was described by Sinatra as the greatest vocal record of the era, although others had commented that Mel's voice was "too pretty" for jazz, and urged him to devote himself to ballads in a lighter vein. For 50 years he excelled in both spheres, maintaining a consistently high standard even when his career was enduring more ups and downs than a Coney Island rollercoaster—a ride described with affecting candor in his autobiography *It Wasn't All Velvet*.

The comparisons with Sinatra are inevitable and revealing. Both men were their own harshest critics and both found jazz fans begrudging in their praise, despite turning in performances that demonstrated a technique and instrumental precision that would be the envy of any self-respecting soloist.

Although he is renowned for taking his songs slow and easy, Mel took his first steps in the music business at a run. Born on September 13, 1925, in Chicago, he was just four years old when he began singing on the radio with the Coon-Sanders Orchestra. From the age of seven he was already proficient on the drums and had a second career rolling as a child actor in radio soaps, which continued until his early teens. During the war years his career gathered momentum as he began writing hit songs for other performers, including "Lament to Love" for Dick Haymes and "Chestnuts Roasting on an Open Fire" for Nat King Cole.

He also studied piano and composition, which eventually led to him writing his own arrangements, an unprecedented achievement for a "popular" singer.

From 1942–43 he toured with a band led by Chico Marx, and from 1943–46 he fronted his own vocal group the Mel-Tones, with whom he had his first hits, while at the same time recording as a soloist with Artie Shaw. But, becoming increasingly frustrated with the lack of creative freedom in both settings, he went solo and almost immediately landed the first of more than a dozen light dramatic roles in the Hollywood musicals *Good News* (1947) and *Words and Music* (1948).

More hits followed on Capitol between 1949 and 1952, including the No. 1 "Careless Hands" and a duet, "The Old Master Painter," with Peggy Lee. The omens were impressive and everything seemed peachy until he was talked into playing the Copacabana club in New York before he felt he was ready for it. He bombed, and had to claw his way back up through the early 50s.

The year 1955 brought a new recording contract with Bethlehem, with whom he really opened up and found his own style, dispeling the famous "fog" and extending his vocal range by another octave.

Mel had been raised on the great song stylists such as Billie Holiday, Frank Sinatra, and Bing Crosby, whose innate musicality inspired him to approach every performance as if he had to convince the listener of his sincerity. He rarely set a pace only to sit back and let the song unwind on its own momentum. Instead, he often set the scene in the first verse and allowed it to build, giving the listener the impression that he was confiding in them, even sharing his most intimate feelings.

Among his finest recordings are "It's a Blue World" (1955), "Mel Tormé Swings Shubert Alley" (1960), "That's All" (1964), and "The Duke Ellington and Count Basie Songbooks" (1961, the latter having strong soloists, sympathetic arrangements, and a choice of the Duke's less familiar material. But even into the 1980s, Mel was still going strong. The first of his tasteful collaborations with pianist George Shearing,"'An Evening with George Shearing and Mel Tormé," garnered a Grammy in 1982, while the similarly titled "An Evening With . . ." saw the magic undimmed as late as 1996. A perfectionist, Tormé was famously intolerant of what he considered the commercial anti-music represented by rock'n'roll and most pop music since. He died in June 1999 after complications resulting from a stroke.

An interview from June 20, 1964, by Max Jones, conducted at a time when, ironically, Tormé had recently enjoyed chart success on both sides of the Atlantic with "Comin' Home Baby."

BEATLES? IT'S A PUT-ON —AND THEY KNOW IT

"Ask me who my favorite female singer is, just for fun." Mel Tormé, in Britain for a BBC 2 recording, was drinking tea and talking in his hotel suite on the London Hilton's lofty 24th floor.

Normally I don't ask singers what they think of other singers unless they want to tell me. Tormé had such an urge, so I said "Who?"

"My absolute favorite vocalist is quite probably unknown in this country. She's little enough known in my country. Name ten female singers and you probably won't get it."

Ella? No. . . . Sarah? No. . . . Betty Carter? "I don't think I know her."

I went through seven or eight names without drawing enthusiasm, then Carmen McRae evoked a response.

"Yes, I like Carmen but she's not my favorite. You won't guess. Jackie Cain! She's unbelievable. She has everything—purity, beauty, musicianship, really paying attention to the lyrics, and singing them incredibly in tune.

"I've never heard Jackie sing a note out of tune. You know, they say you can't sing every note in tune. Well, she can. I've been a fan of hers and her husband's—Roy Kral—for many years.

"Can I say something about singing and improvisation? One of the joys of being a jazz singer is to try to maintain a consistently improvisational approach toward what you sing.

"But—and there's an important but—only if you never lose sight of the original musical values the composer intended. And if you don't

sacrifice the most important element in any popular song—the lyric.

"Aside from these provisions, it's worth remembering that when a singer becomes too involved with improvisation, the improvisation itself palls. Whereas, if you sing a few improvised phrases, they stand out.

"Before we leave the subject of female signers, I should say that in addition to Jackie and Carmen, I think Eydie Gorme has a lot of talent. Peggy Lee—I have to like her; and Barbara McNair is singing very well just now."

Tormé has been a professional for a good many years now. Did he, I asked, tend to look on music as a business these days?

He removed his attention from a TC model MG nipping through the park below ("I had one of the first of those to be made, you know"), and shook his head.

Right: Mel Tormé, photographed by William Claxton in the studio in 1963, in the wake of his only US chart hit "Comin' Home Baby," which also made the best-sellers list in the UK.

Above: Working on
an arrangement with
UK vibes player and
pianist Bill Le Sage
during rehearsals for a
BBC television special
in the early 60s.

"I'm not at that point yet. I have to tell you that as a human mechanism and not a machine, my singing is affected considerably by, say, my domestic life or whatever affects me personally.

"But I have attained enough technique to pull off what the public probably thinks is a good performance, although I know it is not. I mean, I have enough experience to do that.

"So far as the jazz-singer label goes: I think I can count myself a jazz singer, although I don't like the labels. I don't care for labels like jazz, even. "Swing" . . . I like that word, because I know what it means.

"And I know some nights, if I get inspired, I go out and sing a thing and wish to hell I could repeat it. But I can't retain it. I sing it for the moment. It's like quicksilver to me.

"I feel sure about this: if music is the same every night, it's not jazz. Take a performance like the famous Glenn Miller 'In the Mood,' or one of the others. It had to be played the same, right down to the last solo. I can't for the life of me see how that can be jazz.

"Now Artie Shaw, you know he was a good improviser when you hear those albums of radio broadcasts and compare them with more commercial recordings of the same songs. Artie simply played differently every night.

"Yes, I like and admire Shaw, and I think he likes me. We meet still, and have long talks. He's one of the few really intelligent jazz musicians I know. My old records with Artie? I'm pretty proud of them."

In the past, Tormé has been known to complain about disk jockeys, popular songs, and the music biz in general. How does he feel about the situation now?

"Well, to begin with, things are better for me since my 'Coming Home Baby' hit. It opened a lot of doors, no question about it.

"So far as the deejays are concerned, I'd say I was one of the 20 most played artists in America. They're just playing the hell out of me, thank God.

"As for the present beat scene, and America's reaction to some of your young groups, I don't believe that Americans think of it on national lines at all, not any more.

"Rock'n'roll was indigenous to us to begin with, but now it's international, like most popular music. Whether a record is by the Singing Nun or a Japanese boy or an English group, they don't give that a second thought.

"We're in such a faddish age that if something came out by the Dalai Lama of Tibet, and they liked it, they'd buy it. It's sort of a frantic effort to be entertained.

"The Beatles, now, I'd say Americans think of the Beatles as theirs as much as yours. The Beatles give me kind of a kick, not musically, because I won't be hypocritical and say I think it musically, but because I think it's a put-on and they know it.

"And they look nice fellows."

An interview with Mel by Max Jones, published June 17, 1967.

TORMÉ—MEET THE WIFE
IN A SETTING OF BIG BAND ARRANGEMENTS

Two crash helmets bearing the name Honda were the first and least expected objects to catch my eye when I entered the hall of Mel Tormé's London hotel suite.

The singer is known to be a sports car fancier with a taste for elderly MGs and such. But why the lid?

Below: Mel rehearses in a BBC recording studio in Piccadilly, London, during a visit to Britain in July 1956.

ARRANGEMENT

"They're for my motorcycle," Tormé explained. "I've got it outside. It's the best thing to ride in town. We've got two of them at home, and Jan and I both ride them.

"I have an arrangement with the Honda people, and they let me have one wherever we go. They shipped this down from Nottingham when I got here.

"My car is still the old favorite, an SS 100 Jag."

Jan, of course, is Mrs. Tormé—also known as actress Janette Scott.

CONDUCTING

"We work together semi-constantly, but she isn't a regular part of the act. When the whim takes us, I bring her on as a guest and she sings a medley of 16 songs with me at the piano. We sing against each other, eight bars of each song, and finish up in harmony, in thirds, you know. I call it the 'Whoopee' medley. We'll be doing it on my BBC TV show."

Besides being an excellent singer, Tormé is a songwriter, arranger, and pianist who can turn his hand to comedy, acting, conducting, drumming, and picking the baritone ukulele. In other words, he's an accomplished musician as well as an all-rounder.

COMPOSITION

In the line of composition, he is known for his 1949 "California Suite" and such songs as "Stranger in Town," "The Christmas Song," "County Fair," and "After the Waltz Is Over"—the last having been written in this country and recorded with Cyril Stapleton's orchestra.

"I'm still very interested in composing. "The Jet Set," the song I open with at Talk of the Town, is one of mine. Another I wrote is 'Tracy,' about my little boy. I did that on a TV show last time I was here, but I'm not sure if they used it when the program went out.

"My latest record, as a matter of fact, is of my most recent song. It's called "The King,' and it will be released shortly as a single in America."

PRESENTED

Latterly, Tormé has presented himself in a setting of his own big-band arrangements. And he's brought a batch with him for the Burt Rhodes orchestra at the Talk.

"I've done all the charts except 'Foggy Day.' That's an old one by Marty Paich. My most recent arrangement is 'Hey, Look Me Over,' and I've written the chart of 'Mad Mad World.' It begins as a waltz and becomes a real cooker. I think you'll like it.

FLATTERING

"I guess I am rather proud of these charts, and a lot of guys in the bands I've worked with have been crazy about them. It's flattering that they should like them.

"As you may know, I had no training in composition or arranging; no study, no nothing like that. I just learned by trying it out, by applying myself to it. I made mistakes, picked myself up, and I intend to go on."

CREATIVE

I was curious to know, in view of his broad musical interests, whether Tormé continued to find singing artistically satisfying.

"Not really," he said at once. "It's very nice to receive the accolade as a performer. It's good fun to hear the applause.

"But I get a hell of a lot more kick out of the more creative side of my talents, out of songwriting and arranging. It's more lasting, and finally more rewarding."

Above and left:
The camera of John
Hopkins captures
Tormé performing
at the Newport Jazz
Festival, Newport,
Rhode Island, in 1964.

key recordings

1941   Mel's song *"Lament To Love"* was a Top 10 hit for Dick Haymes and Harry James.

1945-6   Debut recordings with Artie Shaw and his own vocal group, The Mel-Tones. First hit *"I Fall in Love Too Easily"* with Mel-Tones and singer Eugenie Baird. Duet with Bing Crosby on *"Day by Day."*

1945   Mel scores another hit when his song *"A Stranger in Town"* is covered by Martha Tilton.

1946   Nat King Cole records *"Christmas Song (Chestnuts Roasting On An Open Fire)."*

1947   *"It's Dreamtime,"* a hit with the Mel-Tones on Majestic.

1947   Classic ballad collection *"Born to Be Blue"* LP.

1949-52 Solo hits on Capitol, including *"Careless Hands"* (No 1) and Top 10 singles *"Bewitched"* with arranger Pete Rugolo.

1950s   Bethlehem LPs include a tribute to Fred Astaire, *"Sings Fred Astaire"* (with arranger Marty Paich), and *"It's a Blue World."*

1950   Mel duets with Peggy Lee *"The Old Master Painter."*

1956   Mel is nominated for an Emmy as best supporting actor for his role as Mickey Rooney's brother in Playhouse 90's *"The Comedian."*

1956   A surprise UK hit for his single *"Mountain Greenery."*

1960   *"Mel Tormé Swings Shubert Alley"* on Verve proves a fine example of the collaboration between Mel and arrangers Paich and Dektette. Tracks include *"Just in Time"* and *"Too Close for Comfort."*

1960   Atlantic LPs included *"Live at the Maisonette"* featuring Gershwin arrangements and received a Grammy nomination.

1961   *"The Duke Ellington and Count Basie Songbooks"* finds Mel in the company of arranger Johnny Mandel and consummate jazz musicians, including Frank Rosolino, Teddy Edwards, and Joe Maini. Highlights include *"I Like the Sunrise"* and Ellington's *"Reminiscing In Tempo"* for which Mel supplied new lyrics.

1962   *"Comin' Home Baby"* LP, title track becomes a Top 40 hit.

1982   *"In New York"* recorded live with the Mike Renzi trio.

1982   *"An Evening with George Shearing and Mel Tormé"* wins a Grammy.

1985   *"An Elegant Evening,"* again with Shearing.

1988   *"In Concert in Tokyo"* reunited Mel with Paich and Dektette.

1990   *"Mel and George Do World War II"* with Shearing.

1992   Tormé teams up with Cleo Laine and John Dankworth for *"Nothing without You."*

1992   *"The Great American Songbook"* on Telarc issued to coincide with an extensive US tour.

1994   *"A Tribute to Bing Crosby"* with Alan Broadbent on piano.

In 1981, at the age of 70, Big Joe Turner, "The Boss of the Blues," discharged himself from a Los Angeles hospital where he had been treated for pneumonia and blood clots and made his way across several states to take the stage at a celebrated nightclub in New York.

Drawing himself up to his full height of 6 ft 2in, Big Joe gripped the microphone as warmly as he would the neck of a bottle of bourbon, and let rip in a buzzsaw baritone that shook the walls, rattled the plates, and rocked the patrons' tables. Big Joe was so named not because of his intimidating build (he weighed in at consistent 250 lbs during his adult years), but for the size of his voice, the full force of which was surely strong enough to register on the Richter scale.

Rock and blues fans have attempted to claim him as their own with some justification. Joe had early crossover hits with seminal R&B sides such as "Chains of Love," "Lipstick, Powder, and Paint" and the original version of "Shake, Rattle, and Roll." But from the early 1950s he regularly revisited his first love—jazz—reaffirming his vows in the illustrious company of Count Basie, Dizzy Gillespie, Joe Newman, and Lawrence Brown.

Joe was born on May 18, 1911, in Kansas City where, at the age of 14, he began as a bartender with a sideline in singing the blues. At the same joint he met and teamed up with his long-time partner-to-be, pianist Pete Johnson, and the pair toured and recorded together through the 1930s and 40s. They attracted attention at John Hammond's Spirituals to Swing concert in 1938, and secured a recording contract with Vocalion, for whom they cut Joe's self-penned "Roll 'em Pete" (later covered by Count Basie) and other seminal sides. Subsequent sessions saw Joe paired with Chicago jazz pianist Joe Sullivan, bandleader Benny Carter, and with the immortal Art Tatum, before he was rewarded with his first solo national R&B hit, "Still in the Dark" in 1950.

A move to Atlantic the following year brought more hits, including "Chains Of Love," "Honey Hush," the double sided "Corrina Corrina"/"Lipstick, Powder, and Paint," and the

record with which he found national fame in 1954, "Shake, Rattle, and Roll." But his thunder was stolen by Bill Haley, who had a national smash with a watered-down version of the song the same year, and later by Elvis Presley, who sounded equally lame by comparison. Joe's volcanic performance of the song in the film of the same name alongside Fats Domino in 1956 must have shaken some of the Greasers down to their drainpipes, but it was clear that the 45-year-old blues shouter was unmarketable as a white teen idol.

His true affiliations were revealed on the 1956 album for Atlantic, "The Boss of the Blues," which was more accurately subtitled "Joe Turner Sings Kansas City Jazz." It was arguably his finest moment, on which his forceful drive and unadorned delivery recalled Bessie Smith in her prime.

His jazz credentials earned him a place at Monterey and other festivals around the world through the 60s and 70s, although his habit of setting fire to hotel rooms drove some of the less understanding promoters to distraction.

For a man with a reputedly limited musical vocabulary (his preference for the key of C is legendary) his later albums on Pablo, Arhoolie, and Muse still packed a punch that would have floored many of the bantam weight R&B groups of the 60s.

Big Joe Turner, the genial giant of jazz singing, died on November 23, 1985, just months after jamming with soulmate Jimmy Witherspoon.

From the boogie-based duets with Pete Johnson in the 30s, through Kansas City small groups to the rhythm and blues outfits that heralded the rock'n'roll revolution, Joe Turner's blues style spanned the worlds of classic jazz and modern pop music.

The interview with Joe Turner, March 1965, appeared under the banner "Kansas City Revisited," one of three pieces devoted to a "Jazz from Kansas City" package tour also featuring such jazz luminaries as Ben Webster, Buck Clayton, Vic Dickenson, and Ruby Braff, and the British outfit backing Joe himself on more than one occasion, the Humphrey Lyttelton Band.

THAT TOWN WAS REALLY ON FIRE, SAYS BIG JOE

After several false alarms, Kansas City's Big Joe Turner has finally made it to Britain—to tour with Buck Clayton and Humphrey Lyttelton's band.

Promoters have been trying to get Turner over here for years.

He was reported to be coming to Britain in 1960 with Big Maybelle, and again later that same year—and I wondered why all the trips had eventually fallen through.

"Well, I don't know," says Joe. "I suppose it's because I don't like to fly. I ain't really stuck on that. Boats? They'd be just as bad. I'd probably be seasick and be in even worse shape.

"Of course I've been to Europe, you know, but never made it here before. I was in Europe with Pete Johnson, my old buddy, for Norman Granz at the time of the Brussels World Fair.

"Since then, I haven't worked much with Pete. We played a couple of concerts for John Hammond up in Newport. I haven't seen Pete in quite a while now."

Johnson was Joe Turner's partner in the old wide-open days of Kansas City, and one way and another they worked together from about 1926 until the middle 40s.

"Me and Pete, we started together at the Sunset—though I met him before that at a place named the Kingfish, and we stuck together a long time. He was a fine boogie woogie player.

"We used to play 'Roll 'em Pete' then, in the Sunset, and that was the first record I ever made—'Roll 'em Pete' and 'Goin' Away Blues,' with Pete in 1938. Yes, they were good days."

How good was the Kansas City musical scene in the 30s?

Below: Joe belts out the blues during a BBC television special *Jazz 625* broadcast from London in early 1965.

Right: Pictured In a
typically relaxed mode,
Turner waiting for the
musicians to set up
their equipment in
preparation for the BBC
Jazz 625 program.

"Oh, it was really jumping.

"There was music all the time, and we had some pretty wild cats out there. Of course, there was Count Basie's band and Andy Kirk's, and Jimmie Lunceford was often there.

"And Julia Lee . . . she and her brother, George, they used to have a good band. And all the musicians used to play at the Sunset one time or another, you know, people like Mary Lou Williams and Ben Webster.

"Yes, Ben's from Kansas City all right, though I haven't seen Mary Lou in a long time.

"That town was really on fire, bouncing. I ain't never found no town like that since. So I think this Kansas concert was a nice idea."

In spite of his affection for old KC, Turner lives nowadays in the city of New Orleans.

Above: Joe on the set of the 1965 BBC TV broadcast.

Above Right: Turner, still taking care of business during the 1970s, preferred the climate in California.

"I got a little house down there; I thought it would make a change. My mother lives out in California and I used to live there. But I've been in New Orleans maybe three years now.

"I kind of like it. There's a lot of good soul food there, you know, 'honey hush' food."

When did Big Joe first learn about blues?

"I started as a little boy.

"I used to carry a blind man around when I was about ten. He was a guitar player, and I used to make up songs to go with it. I guess I been making them up ever since then.

"I used to write a lot of songs, most of the blues I sang were mine. I don't do it so much now. No, I don't know why. I guess I lost the urge."

How does Joe feel about today's blues?

"Truthfully, the trend is changing back and forth so much you don't know which way it's going.

"You have to stay up with the times, that's for sure, but on the other hand, if you change your pattern the public don't like it.

"I try to stick to my pattern because if I change it too much, and ad lib, some one will say afterwards: 'I didn't come here to hear that.'

"Of course, a lot of times I get carried away.

"Then people come back and say I'm not doing the number the way that I used to.

"And I say: 'Yes, well, we made a few changes that time.' It's hard to please everybody."

I told Turner I felt sure he'd please his audiences in Britain.

"Well, I'll try," he said, but somewhat doubtfully, "but I don't guarantee anything.

"It took me so long to get over here, that now everybody's been here before me."

Above: Val Wilmer photographed Joe Turner at home on Cimarron Boulevard, Los Angeles, April 1976.

key recordings

1938 Joe's first recording, *"Roll 'em Pete,"* released with partner, pianist Pete Johnson; later covered by Joe Williams and Count Basie in 1955.

1950 First R&B hit *"Still in the Dark."*

1951-2 More hits with Van "Piano Man" Walls, including *"Chains of Love"* and *"Sweet Sixteen."* Walls had written *"Chains"* with Atlantic boss Ahmet Ertegun.

1953 *"Honey Hush"* released, but it makes its biggest impact entering the Top 60 when reissued in 1959.

1954-6 *"T.V. Mama"* album on which Joe was backed by the Elmore James band.

1954 *"Shake, Rattle, and Roll"* peaks at No. 2 on the R&B chart, followed by the double A side *"Corrine, Corrine"*/*"Lipstick, Powder, and Paint."* *"Corrine"* was adapted from a traditional tune, and Big Joe's biggest pop hit, scraping the Top 40.

1956 Classic Kansas City Jazz set *"Boss of the Blues"* album appeared as Joe was making his screen appearance in the rock movie *Shake, Rattle, and Roll*.

1960 *"Singing the Blues"* album on Impulse

1972 *"Flip, Flop, and Fly"* recorded live in Frankfurt and Paris with Basie.

1974 Film documentary *Last of the Blue Devils* features a jam session reunion at the Kansas City Musicians Union hall, with Turner, Count Basie, Jay McShann, and other legendary figures from the KC scene.

1974 *"Stormy Monday"* LP featuring Dizzy Gillespie, Roy Eldridge, and Eddie Vinson.

1974-6 A series of LPs for Norman Granz's Pablo label includes *"The Bosses"* with Basie and *"Kansas City Here I Come"* with Basie and Eddie Vinson.

1983 Joe jams with Dr. John (Mac Rebennack) and Roomful of Blues on the album *"Blues Train."*

With her innate sense of swing and gift for improvisation, Sarah Vaughan surely qualified as the archetypal jazz singer, although she disliked being categorized as such.

The possessor of a four-octave range and near-perfect pitch, she had the potential to be an opera diva, but prided herself on never having sung a song the same way twice—a habit that would not have endeared her to operatic impresarios.

While jazz fans and critics honored her with the appellation "The Divine One," in acknowledgment of her classical qualities, her fellow musicians preferred the nickname "Sassy," in celebration of her earthier attributes.

Although untutored, she was a consummate musician with a natural rhythmic flair, an easygoing manner, and an impeccable ear for harmony that enabled her spontaneously to recompose a melody line in performance. On the rare occasions when she chose to scat she could out-bop Ella Fitzgerald. Her tone, too, was as expansive as her vocal range, opening up from a warm, intimate sensuality to a ringing soprano that could shake the chandeliers in Carnegie Hall.

Sarah was born in Newark, New Jersey, on March 27, 1924. As a child, she studied piano, which gave her an extensive harmonic vocabulary from which she was to enrich her vocal lines. Her initial performances were confined to singing in church, then in 1943 she took a chance to prove herself in front of a discriminating audience on amateur night at Harlem's Apollo Theater. Needless to say, she won, and within days was recruited by bandleader Earl Hines on the recommendation of his singer Billy Eckstine, who had been in the audience when Sarah made her debut. Billy became her mentor and inspiration and so, when he split from Hines in 1944 to form his own band, Sarah inevitably followed.

Within a year she was recording timeless tunes such as "Tenderly," "It's You or No One," and "Time and Again" under her own name in a popular romantic manner somewhat similar to Billy's. At the peak of her popular success (1954-66), she notched up 20 hit singles,

Left: An evocative shot of "Sassy," as Sarah Vaughan was known, by the master of jazz photography Herman Leonard, taken in New York City in 1948.

Right: In rehearsal, Sarah in the 1960s, captured on camera by Chuck Stewart.

including a duet with Eckstine, "Passing Strangers," and three Top 10 singles "Whatever Lola Wants," "Make Yourself Comfortable," and "Broken-Hearted Melody."

These won over a substantial middle-of-the-road audience, whose interest prompted her to record with orchestras who were more often than not strictly mainstream. The easy-listening arrangements scored by Hal Mooney for her albums of Gershwin standards in the mid 50s, for example, were far too bland and anonymous for a singer of Sarah's jazz capabilities, swamping both singer and song in a gluttonous morass of syrupy strings. But even in such unsympathetic settings, her innate musicality saw her through. Her performances have always been an object lesson in how to put a song across with a finesse and refined musicality, which few popular singers of the time possessed.

Fortunately, for many of her live performances and her classic early 60s Roulette recordings, "After Hours" and "Plus Two," she chose to work out with a small coterie of jazz musicians, including her long-time partner, the pianist Jimmy Jones, drummers Roy Haynes and Jimmy Cobb, master guitarist Mundell Lowe, and bass player George Duvivier. The more intimate setting allowed Sarah the space to stretch out and show how she could turn even the most familiar standard inside out, with all the dynamic grandeur and subtle shadings of a small symphony orchestra.

Sarah Vaughan passed away on April 3, 1990, in Los Angeles, leaving behind a legacy of recordings that attest to her status as a supreme jazz diva.

Max Jones interviewed Sarah Vaughan after she had completed two concert dates in London in January 1960, on which she was accompanied by the prestigious UK big band, the Johnny Dankworth Orchestra.

PLEASE DON'T TYPE ME !

Jazz singers, like other artists, enjoy success. They like having hit records, and the earnings these bring.

Sarah Vaughan is no exception.

"Broken-Hearted Melody" has brought her to a wider public than ever, although it is not too popular with the jazz audience, which—perhaps understandably—distrusts commercial success.

A danger inherent in hit records is that the gifted performer may be tempted to concentrate on potential money-makers instead of giving rein to her proper talents.

Sarah is aware of the dilemma, and she hopes that she has found a way out of it.

"I have two record contracts," she told me. "One for jazz albums, the other for commercial things. Both with Mercury."

It looks like a sensible compromise, but does Sarah find herself making more and more of the "commercial things"?

She says no, pointing out that as you never know what makes big-sellers, you cannot turn them out to order.

"Sometimes you record an album and one particular track becomes a favorite with the public. Then the company snatches it out and makes it a single. On the other hand, when your singles slow down on sales they often get put into albums.

REQUESTS

"You just never know what's going to happen when you make a record. My contract stipulates so many sides a year, no less. But I can always make extra albums if there's something I want to do. So there's no question of one type of record squeezing out the other."

I asked Sarah if she felt obliged to feature a current hit, such as "Broken-Hearted Melody," at all her performances.

She thought about this, and explained: "I love the fact that people ask for any of my recorded songs. I like to sing their requests. But can

Above: Sarah Vaughan
backstage, playing
solo cards in her
dressing room.

Left: A glossy publicity
shot from the early
1950s.

you imagine singing the same song at every show in every town in all the different countries?

"It does get a little monotonous, but when you're obligated to people you really have no choice. Look at it this way. The reason you have a hit is because people like the song and buy the record. Then that's the first thing they demand to hear. What are you going to do?"

Obligations apart, what music would Sarah Vaughan herself choose to sing?

"I am trying to get away from being typed as a jazz artist," she said, "though I'm not going to stop singing jazz.

"After all, there are so many music lovers in this world. I cannot reach them all because I don't sing every style of music. But I try to reach as many as I can

BALLADS

"My heart really lies with the pretty ballads. For that matter, I like good tunes of every description. I'd love to do a whole album of spirituals, other folk songs, too.

"There are more things I'd like to do—a revue, and a TV show of my own. One day, I hope . . .

"But I realize this: if I did only the things I love doing. I'm sure I wouldn't have all the fans I have now."

A great many of Sarah's London admirers went to the Festival Hall last Saturday and the Finsbury Park Astoria on Sunday, and gave her a warm reception.

ARTISTRY

She in turn gave an exhibition of vocal artistry that could hardly be faulted at any point. Certainly it was the greatest sitting-down concert we are ever likely to see.

And, as proof that she is not inflexible about her current hit songs, Sarah included "Broken-Hearted Melody" on Saturday, but left it out the next day.

I thought her program was better without it.

The *Melody Maker*'s main man jazz-wise, Max Jones, spoke to Sarah again in an interview published on September 21, 1963, when she was visiting Britain with a new backing trio.

MADAME BUTTERFLY

MAX JONES TALKS TO A NEW-LOOK SARAH VAUGHAN

Each time Sarah Vaughan works here I seem to write about a new-look Sarah with a fresh line in presentation.

This time we again see a restyled singer. Visually, a fugitive touch of Madame Butterfly, and a host of newly acquired gestures and motions gratify the eye.

Vocally, she is as splendid as ever. But various expressive nuances match her stage manner and contribute to this latest, more frolicsome Vaughan image.

INNOVATIONS

A few of the comedy innovations may leave her old-school followers cold. But I feel sure the majority of concertgoers will find her act agreeably relaxed and friendly.

Sarah told me that the changes had come about gradually since the time we saw her last.

"You know, the singing and presentation have to alter over the years, just as a performance changes from concert to concert. When you've sung a song for ten years, what else can you do?"

139

Below: On stage during a tour of US army camps, in Mildenhall, England, with Joe Benjamin on bass and tenor sax giants Coleman Hawkins and Illinois Jacquet.

About the new trio: "You like my trio? Fine. Of course they influence what I do; musicians always give me ideas.

"They are young musicians, kind of inspiring. My bass player, Charles Williams, gives me ideas the whole time. And Kirk Stuart's always creating something on stage. I like to work that way."

Because of her extraordinary instrumental quality, and control of tone and vibrato, Sarah has often been likened to horn players. Was she inspired by trumpet players?

"Well," she answered somewhat evasively, "I can think of a couple of trumpet players who inspire me right now."

I asked about her vibrato, which varies so much from song to song, from one register to another sometimes. As a rule, she employs less vibrato for ballads than for jazz tunes.

I wondered whether these variations were conscious or instinctive.

"I guess you'd have to say instinctive. It's just the way it comes out. It varies according to the story of the song and the arrangement. That's all I can tell you."

Does she think much in advance about a treatment, and work on it, and does she practice at all?

"So far as practicing goes, I think about it more than do it. I don't often rehearse, and I work enough to keep my voice in shape."

IT ALL FITS

"The treatment of a song, well, I say, it's according to the feel of the song and the arrangement it's given. You have to know what the arranger has in mind before you decide how to do it.

"With some arrangers, like Benny Carter and Quincy Jones, Robert Farnon and Lalo Schifrin, you find that when you get a recording date everything you do fits into place.

"I did a date with Lalo Schifrin not long ago and we had time to get together and work things over. I enjoyed that. Lalo writes very well, and when a musician writes well that gives me ideas, too.

"When we finish in Britain we go back to Copenhagen to make an album with Robert Farnon. He's writing and conducting the session. I dig his work so much."

Sarah was quoted recently as saying she was getting set to do a concert series with symphony orchestras in the States, then maybe in Europe. Any progress to report?

"It was just a thought," she admitted. "I want very much to do something like that, something different from jazz and popular songs.

"It's still an idea in my mind, and it might happen . . . but not yet. What would I sing? Like classics, spirituals maybe, and some good standards from different countries—sung in English, you know, or perhaps without words."

DOUBLE SIX

"Things like this . . . " Here, Sarah launched her soprano voice gently on "One Fine day" from *Madame Butterfly*, You'll travel a long way to meet such warm, pure tone and accurate pitching.

In Paris the other week she had been knocked out by Les Double Six, the remarkable French vocal group.

"What a group, they're nuts," she enthused.

"I'm telling you, I couldn't sing with them if I was in that group. They should go to the States now and get real recognition.

"I'm sure they will."

Left: The divine Sarah flanked by admirer and fellow artist Mel Tormé and long-time colleague Billy Eckstine.

Above: Sarah Vaughan in rehearsal for a recording session in 1950, New York City.

Above right: From the same session, Sarah in stocking feet runs through a score.

1944 Sarah joined Earl Hines after being spotted by Billy Eckstine at an Apollo Amateur Night contest.

1946-9 Sarah joined Eckstine as featured female vocalist, recording songs such as *"It's You or No One," "Tenderly,"* and *"Time and Again."*

1954-7 *"Swingin' Easy"* LP compiled from two sessions featuring Sarah with her regular trios. Includes her justly celebrated *"Shulie A Bop,"* her scat version of *"Summertime,"* and a cover of *"Lover Man."*

1954 *"Sarah Vaughan with Clifford Brown"*—a classic meeting with the ill-fated trumpet legend Clifford Brown marked Sarah's first 100 percent proof jazz session after a decade as a pop vocalist. Includes *"Lullaby Of Birdland"* and *"You're Not The Kind."*

1954 The Top 10 singles *"Make Yourself Comfortable"* and *"Whatever Lola Wants"* begin a string of 20 hit singles between 1954 and 1966.

1954 *"Sarah Vaughan"* LP.

1954-8 *"The Rodgers and Hart Songbook"* LP.

1955 *"In the Land of Hi-Fi"* with Cannonball Adderley and Ernie Wilkins.

1955 *"Sarah Vaughan In Hi-Fi"* LP (not to be confused with the *"In the Land of Hifi"* album) featured Sarah with Miles Davis.

1956 *"Linger Awhile"* album on Columbia goes Top 20; it was released in the same year in which she was enjoying single success with Mercury.

1957 A duet single with Eckstine, *"Passing Strangers,"* is a hit on Mercury.

1957 *"Sarah Vaughan and Billy Eckstine Sing the Best of Irving Berlin"* LP.

1959 The single *"Broken-Hearted Melody"* becomes another hit.

1959 *"Sings George Gershwin"* arranged by Hal Mooney.

1960s Albums for Roulette included *"The Explosive Side of Sarah Vaughan"* and *"The Lonely Hours,"* later reissued on CD as *"The Benny Carter Sessions."*

1960-1 *"No Count Sarah"* puts Sarah with the Basie Band (and duetting with Joe Williams on two tracks), although the Count himself does not put in an appearance.

1961 *"After Hours"* LP finds Sarah in session with George Duvivier and Mundell Lowe, laying down superlative readings of *"In a Sentimental Mood"* and *"My Favorite Things."*

1962 *"You're Mine You"* with Quincy Jones.

1964 *"The Lonely Hours"* included *"The Man I Love"* and *"These Foolish Things."*

1970s Sarah joined the Duke for *"The Duke Ellington Songbook"* series of LPs.

1982 *"Crazy and Mixed Up"* album was just one of a string of latter day successes. A mix of standards and new songs with backing from Roland Hanna's quartet. Sarah selected the musicians and the songs, which include *"Autumn Leaves," "That's All,"* and *"Love Dance."*

1982 A later highlight came with *"Gershwin Live"* with the LA Philharmonic conducted by Michael Tilson Thomas.

1986 Sarah sings in a studio recording of *"South Pacific,"* with Dame Kiri Te Kanawa and José Carreras.

142 dinah washington

"Queen D," or the "Divine Miss D," as many prefer to call her, was blessed with one of the most distinctive voices in popular music—a smoky vibrato which was equally at ease with gospel, jazz, or blues. She can be credited with bringing the fluid phrasing of gospel (known as melisma) to secular popular music—pre-empting Ray Charles by a decade. Her sinewy intonation and strident style influenced and inspired many of the major female jazz and soul singers over the following four decades, most notably Aretha Franklin, Esther Phillips, and Nancy Wilson.

Dinah's royal appellation was bestowed on her by fellow performers with a hint of irony, for her queenly status as an artist was matched by her imperious behavior toward those she feared would upstage her. She once demanded that Jimmy Witherspoon be dropped from the bill because there was "too much blues" on the show, and is said to have cut Brook Benton dead whenever she found herself in the same room with him, despite having recorded two hit singles with the singer.

She was frequently short-changed by inferior material that had been imposed on her by various record companies who were desperate for a pop hit, but even on the most unpromising material her sincerity and commitment were total.

Dinah was born Ruth Lee Jones on August 29, 1924, in Tuscaloosa, Alabama. As a teenager she sang lead on a tour with the Chicago-based gospel choir the Sallie Martin Singers, and remained in the Windy City when the tour came to an end. She was working in the Regal Theater as a washroom attendant under her real name when bandleader Lionel Hampton discovered her at the age of 18 and renamed her Dinah Washington.

From 1943–46 she sang with Hampton's orchestra, sharing the vocal spotlight with Joe Williams, and cut her first sides, including "Evil Gal Blues" and "Salty Papa Blues," for the Keynote label with the bandleader's sidemen. Her only recording with the full orchestra, "Blow Top Blues," was not actually issued until she had left the outfit to go solo.

By all accounts, her tenure with Hampton was stormy and fated to be brief. Hampton forbade his musicians to play on other artists' recordings, but he was captivated by Dinah's emotive style of singing, and he sneaked out to play drums and his inimitable two-fingered piano style on one of her early solo sessions. When his formidable wife, Gladys, found out she kicked up so much fuss that Dinah was persuaded to go solo.

Dinah's 15-year reign at Mercury Records began in the late 1940s with a run of R&B hits, including two No. ones, "Am I Asking Too Much" and "Baby Get Lost," which demonstrated a maturity beyond her years. She then branched out into pop under the direction of Mitch Miller, Mercury's in-house producer whose questionable judgment and taste frustrated many of the label's artists. Miller had her record Broadway tunes, and even country songs that were clearly unsuitable and sent her sales into freefall. But her career was resuscitated in 1954 when the label's A&R manager Bob Shad had the bright idea to give her two outlets, separating her pop and R&B output from her jazz albums, which were to be recorded for his new Emarcy subsidiary. These recordings found Dinah in an informal setting reworking a repertoire of aching blues and classic jazz gilded with that yearning, aspiring quality that she brought from her gospel roots.

In 1958, her cross-over career was reclaimed when she was teamed with producer and songwriter Clyde Otis, and she ended the decade as arguably the most popular black female singer of the 1950s.

At the start of the 60s, Otis created three No. one R&B hits for her within six months, two of them duets with Brook Benton and the third her own, "This Bitter Earth."

A switch to Roulette in 1962 brought Washington a few more hits, but apparently it did not compensate for her unsettled private life, which saw her marrying seven times and descending into alcoholism.

Dinah died from a fatal cocktail of drink and pills on December 14, 1963. Always a class act in every sense of the word, Dinah Washington was among a handful of artists who crossed the barrier between jazz and R&B with no compromise in style.

An interview from June 1959 by Max Jones, when Dinah was enjoying fame as a popular jazz-tinged singer in the R&B mold.

DINAH WASHINGTON SAYS—YOU'VE GOT TO HAVE SOUL!

Dinah Washington, the powerful and magnetic singer who America knows as "The Queen," is in Britain for the first time in her life.

She has taped a three-song TV act for Granada's *The Variety Show* (to be seen on July 1), and sung on Thursday's BBC *Jazz Club*. She goes to Sweden in a week.

Installed in her Oxford Street hotel, she telephoned home to New York, poured brandy for the *Melody Maker*, and proposed various robust poses to our photographer.

Her pianist Beryl Booker retired, beat, almost at once. But Dinah scorned a suggestion of rest, and even executed some perky dance steps before talking animatedly about her children.

They are George (12), who plays drums, and Bobby (10), and they have just made their stage debut at New York's Apollo Theater.

"I closed there Thursday night," Dinah explained. "My kids were on, too. They stole the show, and made 125 dollars apiece. If they don't join me here soon I'm likely to get dangerous."

I had heard Dinah was on the fiery side, but I found her friendly and approachable. She is outspoken, as anyone knows who has read her "blindfold tests" for Leonard Feather, but shrewd and humorous.

CONVICTION

I asked Dinah if she regarded herself as a jazz singer, a pop singer, or what.

"I don't think of myself as anything except a singer," she said. "I like to sing, and I'll sing ballads, church songs, blues, anything. I'll sing 'Eli Eli' if you hang around.

"People who call me a blues singer don't understand what I'm doing. I used to specialize in blues with Lionel Hampton's band, and I still sing them. But I'm not restricted to any one kind of song.

"To me, the important thing is soul and conviction. You've got to have a feeling. That 'Backwater Blues' of Bessie's that I did, I had tears in my eyes.

"Someone came up to me right after I'd finished and I had to say: 'I'm sorry. I'll see you later.' Whenever I sing 'Backwater,' my friends practically have to carry me off the stage.

"Bessie Smith? I never saw her, but I listen to her records now and don't hear nothing wrong. She had some good songs, and a crazy piano player, James P. Johnson.

"Rock'n'roll you can have, but I like real blues. 'Backwater Blues' or 'You've Been a Good Old Wagon' . . . you can break loose on those."

I asked Dinah, who used to sing and play piano in church, how she felt about the mixing of blues and gospel qualities.

"I don't know about the mixture as a general thing," she said. "But it sounds all right when Ray Charles sings.

"So far as I'm concerned, it's a source of feeling. It doesn't matter too much what the emotion is: if you've got any kind of feeling—you know, soul?—it'll do.

"I'll tell you what it's like. The Negro has been downtrodden in America for a long time, as you know. Maybe when you're singing a certain song you think of things that happened to you years ago."

COMMENTS

"I've done that, and there's been guys in the audience—who couldn't guess at what you're feeling—that have jumped up in their chairs.

"What I'm saying is, you might not understand the exact emotion, but you feel something, right? Spiritual, blues, ballad, it doesn't matter."

Here are some more of Dinah's comments:

On Ray Charles: "He and I sit up and sing together. You ought to hear us on 'Drown In Your Own Tears.'"

Male singers: "I'll tell you what I like in one sentence: Ray Charles, Frank Sinatra and Nat Cole."

Billie Holiday: "I love her. Perhaps you've heard me mimic her on 'Lover Come Back To Me.'"

Annie Ross: "That's my buddy—she's crazy."

Female pianists: "There's only four women that I say can really play piano . . . Beryl Booker, Martha Davis, Terry Pollard, and Mary Lou. They used to try to get me to play in my act, but I prefer to stand up and pick the customers out."

DISC HIT

On the old "Queen of the Blues" tag: "Call me Queen of the Jukeboxes, honey. I finally got a hit, but I practically had to whip those disk jockeys to get it."

The hit is "What a Difference a Day Makes," released here on EMI's Mercury label this weekend.

"I'll give you something to write about," Dinah said as I was readying to leave. "I love to cook, and I really can do it."

An hour or two later, after some energetic marketing in Soho, an aproned Dinah Washington served up a meal of fried chicken, Lyonnaise potatoes, peas and salad, which proved to my satisfaction that she is also a queen of the kitchen.

147

Above and left: Dinah Washington pictured in the recording studio, photographed by Herman Leonard and Chuck Stewart respectively.

key recordings

1943 Dinah's first recording session under her own name, after singing with Lionel Hampton, was produced by Leonard Feather for Keynote. Tracks included Feather's *"Evil Gal Blues"* and *"Salty Papa Blues"* with Hampton on piano and drums.

1945 Her debut album *"Mellow Man"* boasts Milt Jackson and Charles Mingus among the credits.

1949 First of almost 30 R&B hit singles for Mercury, *"Baby Get Lost,"* was a No, 1. In response Decca, who had earlier turned down Washington, asked Billie Holiday to record a version.

1954 The album *"Dinah Jams"* captures a live studio set featuring jazz giants Clifford Brown, Max Roach, Clark Terry, and Maynard Ferguson.

1957 *"The Fats Waller Songbook"* LP.

1958 *"The Bessie Smith Songbook"* recorded with her current husband, Eddie Chamblee, and a hot Chicago ensemble.

1959 *"What a Difference a Day Makes"* is Dinah's biggest solo single, peaking at No.8 in the US charts.

1960 Dinah's second No.1 was *"This Bitter Earth."* In between her first, *"Baby Get Lost,"* and *"This Bitter Earth"* she had 20 singles on the pop chart, including *"What a Difference a Day Makes," "Our Love Is Here to Stay"* and *"September in the Rain."*

1960 Two duets, *"Baby (You Got What It Takes)"* and *"A Rockin' Good Way (To Mess Around and Fall In Love),"* found her cracking the Top Ten in the company of Brook Benton.

1960 The album *"What a Difference a Day Makes"* hits the charts. The title track had been a hit originally in 1934 for the Dorsey Brothers.

1962 A move to Roulette brought a few more hit singles and the chart albums *"Dinah," "Drinking Again," "Back to the Blues,"* and *"A Stranger on Earth."*

1962 The album *"I Wanna Be Loved"* charted, as did the title track, which was a re-recording of her first pop hit from 1950.

The formidable voice of Joe Williams, Count Basie's frontman in the late 1950s, packed a wallop that could floor lesser men with the impact of a fist in a velvet glove. And yet, despite his popularity over several decades, he is often confused with "Big Joe" Williams, the blues guitarist and singer.

No doubt the confusion was compounded by Joe's occasional forays into R&B, specifically his big hit "Everyday I Have the Blues," and his tendency when interviewed to deny that he was simply a jazz singer. His personal favorite among his own albums was the 1987 LP "Ballad and Blues Master," which is a fair description of his area of influence, although it is probably more accurate to say that he brought the raw power of R&B and popular vocal techniques to jazz.

Joe himself couldn't have cared less for categories or fitting the job description. He was too busy having a good time trading lines with some of the best instrumentalists of his day, and wrapping that cavernous voice of his around songs of lost love and loneliness. As he moved into middle age in the 1960s, his voice mellowed and his performances acquired the honest intimacy of a barfly's confession. Even on record, his considerable presence could be quite intimidating, demanding that you heard him out.

There are those who rate Joe higher than Billy Eckstine ,and who say that his masterly interpretation of Ellington's "Come Sunday" suggests that if he had been smarter and made the move from the Count to the Duke's camp, nobody would be mistaking him for a blues singer today.

Joe was born Joseph Goreed on December 12, 1918, in Cordele, Georgia. By his teens he was already a familiar face in the Chicago clubs, where he was fronting a band led by clarinettist Jimmie Noone, who was to inspire the young Benny Goodman. But the band was too lightweight for Joe, who was shaping up to be a big hitter. He was restless to get in the ring with the heavyweights, and jumped at the chance when it came to join the innovative and highly influential Coleman Hawkins, and go a few rounds with the band with which the Hawk had recorded "Body and Soul." From there it was an inevitable side-step to the Lionel Hampton orchestra, with which he spent much of the early 40s before cutting his first record with Andy Kirk at the end of the decade. He sparred with other outfits such as the Albert Ammons-Pete Johnson band, Red Saunders and Hot Lips Page, and the Count Basie septet, which gave him more stage experience. However, Joe's recording opportunities were scarce until the chance came in 1951 to cut "Everyday I Have the Blues" with backing from the King Kolax R&B band. Although the record brought him to public prominence, his progress was retarded by prejudice from both white club owners and black band leaders, who considered him too dark and earthy for the jazz circuit. Consequently, he toned down his magnificent craggy voice to a timbre reminiscent of Billy Eckstine, with a smattering of showbiz flourishes to please the crowds.

In 1955, he remade "Everyday" with Ella Fitzgerald and Count Basie, who he had joined in 1954, and with whom he stayed until 1960, bringing renewed vigor and a fresh impetus to the band. Joe's contribution to Basie's renewed popularity in this period is not to be underestimated, although his determination to enjoy his tenure with the Count was sometimes at the expense of the song's downbeat theme, giving the impression that, for Joe, the blues was a bittersweet experience.

After Basie, Joe launched a solo career through the 60s and 70s with backing from the Harry Edison quintet, then with his own trios led by Chicago pianists Norman Simmons and Junior Mance. An African tour with the Clark Terry quintet in 1979 found him still in fine voice, and there were also occasional reunions with Basie before Joe found "a steady job" as a TV actor.

Ask a non-jazz fan today who Joe Williams is and you'll probably be told that he played Bill Cosby's father-in-law in the comic's long-running popular TV series. No doubt it paid the bills, but I suspect that Joe would rather have been mistaken for a blues singer than be remembered for that.

Maurice Burman speaks to Joe Williams, February 21, 1959.

I SING THE WAY I FEEL, SAYS JOE WILLIAMS

Backstage at the Festival Hall, as the Basie Band swung into its second show, Joe Williams, in shirt and socks, was changing in his dressing room.

Slipping on his trousers—"I'll get round to the shoes later"—he faced me impassively as I put the following questions:

"Have you ever taken singing lessons?"

"No. I'm not bragging. I probably need them badly. I advise all youngsters to take them and study."

"Some critics suggest you are not a blues singer but a blues-tinged popular singer."

"There's no accounting for how people hear you. I can't comment on that because I don't know how they base their criticism or what they're hearing."

MUMBO JUMBO

"I have never said this to the Press before, but the people of the days of slavery and shortly after had their blues. A lot of it was good. Some of it you couldn't understand and a lot of it was mumbo jumbo.

"We today have the blues, too, but it is a blues of our day. It's more of the mind and heart and not of the beating of the back.

"The blues have more than 12 bars—let no one kid you. 'I Cover The Waterfront' is a blues, too; it's a sound of love, of wailing, and of mixed emotions, and when it's done right, that, too, is good jazz."

"Which do you consider more important—the emotional expression or technical quality?"

"For jazz? One must feel the rule of what one is singing for all music—opera and jazz. Some things I sing are trite.

Right: Joe Williams photographed in expansive action by the great Herman Leonard, New York City, 1954.

"I want to get away from that; but coming back to your question—I really can't say, not being a thorough musician. You sing the way you feel. That's what jazz is and that's why I find it difficult to mime on TV."

NO DISTRACTION

"You are a very great swinging singer. Why then do you stand perfectly still when you sing?"

"I don't give a great deal of thought to this but people might not listen to you if you distract them by moving about."

"Who is your favorite band?"

He smiled broadly: "I'll tell you. The most consistently good and most exciting band is Basie, but on a given night, when the Ellington band is really hot—that's something to listen to. They're my two bands.

"By the way, I would like to say that I'm most grateful to the *Melody Maker* readers for having been mentioned in the Poll. I didn't know I was that popular."

Joe Williams interviewed by Max Jones, September 29, 1962.

IT'S GREAT TO BE COMING BACK SAYS JOE WILLIAMS

Joe Williams, who steps into a concert spot left vacant by an indisposed Sarah Vaughan, is returning to Britain sooner than most of us expected.

Sooner than he expected, too? I asked him over the transatlantic telephone this week.

"Well no, actually." The warm tones came over so clearly that Williams could have been in Temple Bar instead of Toronto. "I expected to be seeing you earlier than this. I almost came over, at least twice, to do television shows in England. I was going to do a week of TV when the disputes with Equity and our union in America put a stop to it.

I'M THRILLED

"Anyhow, now I am on the way, and I'm looking forward to it very, very much. Yes, it was a surprise, and a pleasant one. I look on Britain as a bit of a home, you know that."

But this will be his first appearance here as a single. How does he feel about the new experience?

"I am absolutely thrilled, looking forward to it with happy expectancy because, as I say, I was always so well received.

"And then, too, I have some things I couldn't do before . . ."

The program, I asked, will it emphasize jazz or what?

"Oh, it will be a mixture—swing tunes, blues, and ballads. Some will be old songs, some very new that I haven't even recorded yet."

Accompanying Williams is Julian Clifford (Junior) Mance, the excellent and very blues-conscious Chicago pianist we saw here with Gillespie's quintet in 1959.

"Mance has been with me since the beginning of August, since Harry Edison and I parted company— he's a fine man and piano player."

I asked Joe how he'd been making out professionally since he left Basie in the summer of 1961.

WITH SWEETS

"Forty-six weeks in the last year," he said cheerfully. "Does that answer your question? And I've been able to work with, and pay, Harry Edison's wonderful jazz group."

A final question: is Joe concentrating more on ballads nowadays?

"I don't think so. At present, I'm doing as many blues as I ever did. I like blues, but I think the scope is wider than that, and I'm so glad it is."

152

Below: A 1976 shot of Joe on stage at Carnegie Hall, New York, by noted UK jazz photographer David Redfern.

**Above: Another Redfern
picture, taken at the
Montreux Jazz Festival
in Switzerland in 1972.**

key recordings

1946 After a ten-year apprenticeship singing with Jimmie Noone and Coleman Hawkins, Joe cuts his first record with Andy Kirk.

1951 Breakthrough hit with *"Everyday I Have the Blues"* backed by the King Kolax R&B band.

1955 A year after joining Basie, Joe records the seminal *"Count Basie Swings, Joe Williams Sings"* LP on Verve, including a remake of *"Everyday"* with guest sparring partner Ella Fitzgerald. It was to become one of the most successful jazz albums of the era.

1956 Scat duet *"Party Blues"* with Ella and Basie was the product of a Metronome All-Star session.

1959 Joe joins Lambert, Henricks, and Ross for a remake of the Jimmy Rushing song *"Goin' to Chicago."*

1966 *"Presenting Joe Williams and the Thad Jones-Mel Lewis Orchestra"* album shows that Joe's voice has mellowed like vintage wine with middle age. It includes a truly inspiring reading of Ellington's *"Come Sunday,"* which would have endeared him to the Duke.

1983 *"Nothing but the Blues"* with Jack McDuff, Eddie Vinson, and Ray Brown was greeted with rave reviews.

1987 *"Ballad and Blues Master,"* a live album, has Joe supported by the Norman Simmons trio.

1987 *"Every Night,"* a live LP for Verve, was recorded at the Vine Street Bar & Grill in Hollywood, with a quartet led by pianist Norman Simmons, Joe's regular accompanist for some time.

Jimmy Witherspoon was a blues "shouter" in the Chicago tradition, but he preferred his blues subdued, after-hours style, in the genial company of jazz musicians. His celebrated appearance at the 1959 Monterey Jazz festival saw him sharing the stage with Roy Eldridge, Coleman Hawkins, Woody Herman, Earl "Fatha" Hines, and his old friend Ben Webster, in whose company he would tease the timing and melody of a blues tune with the sensibility and mellifluous phrasing of a jazz singer.

Blessed with a rich baritone, he could belt out the blues or ride a riff with a big band as he did with Jay McShann and Count Basie, but the flexibility and sophisticated sheen for which he was justly celebrated was heard to better effect on mid-tempo ballads such as the 1965 Hot 100 hit "You're Next."

Spoon was a larger-than-life figure who prided himself on being a dapper dude. In the late 1960s he was to be seen sporting a silver-topped cane and elegantly attired in a tailored suit and tie. His hair would be combed back to reveal weathered features framed with long sideburns and a wicked mustache, which seemed to grow more prominent through the years.

"Spoon" was born on August 8, 1923, in Gurdon, Arkansas, where he sang in the local Baptist church choir from the age of seven. He didn't get to grips with the blues until he enlisted in the navy in 1941, where, during docking spells in Calcutta, he started singing blues with a band led by Teddy Weatherford. On demobilization he promptly paid his dues with Jay McShann's eight piece blues 'n' boogie outfit, working the West Coast from 1945–1947. He made his first recordings with McShann and a number of other bands, including the Buddy Tate group and the Roy Milton band, as a featured vocalist and as a solo singer, but the hits were slow in coming.

Success finally came in 1949 with the release of "Ain't Nobody's Business," a slow, lurching 12-bar blues which hit the No. one spot in the R&B chart, but subsequent

Left: "Spoon" in action
toward the end of the
60s at the Nice Jazz
Festival, photographed
by Tim Motion.

singles on Supreme and Modern failed to ignite. Interest tailed off, leaving "Spoon" to languish in near obscurity for much of the 1950s.

A near legendary appearance at the 1959 Monterey Jazz festival with an all-star line-up restored him to favor and brought in the bookings for a succession of European tours, which saw him venerated as a graduate of the authentic Chicago school by the young white blues aficionados. He began to record again for RCA, Atlantic, and Reprise, and made a point of including prisons in his tour schedule.

"Spoon" seemed destined to enjoy a second career for as long as he could hold a mike, but in the early 70s he tired of touring and took a back seat, spinning blues records on the radio. It took the interest of the British blues singer Eric Burdon to coax him out of retirement in order to show the disco generation what they were missing.

In 1975, he had a hit with "Love Is a Five Letter Word," and in 1992 "The Blues, the Whole Blues and Nothin' but the Blues" was a debut release for the Indigo label, founded by the veteran UK blues producer Mike Vernon. "Spoon" toured to considerable acclaim through the 70s and 80s in spite of suffering from throat cancer, from which he never fully recovered. He died in 1997.

Jimmy Witherspoon talks to Max Jones, September 15, 1964.

IT'S STILL THE BLUES

"Do I enjoy working in Europe?" Jimmy Witherspoon—now on his third professional visit to Britain and looking as though he is relishing it—didn't take long to answer the question.

"Yes, I like it very much. I've sung in France, England, Germany, Sweden, and Norway, and enjoyed myself in all of them. And I think the people have enjoyed my singing.

"Certainly I've made many friends, and I've appeared on radio and TV shows which have done me a lot of good. What you get in Europe, when you're a visiting American jazz musician, is recognition—which is what every artist needs. Truthfully, I feel I've had more recognition here in Europe than at home. But, old as I am, what I need as well is money."

How does Jimmy feel about the popular music he hears in Britain?

"In the first place, it's no different from what I hear at home, no different from the Top 50 in the States.

"So far as your beat groups go, I think most of them—like the Beatles—are trying to sing the blues. But they've got their own way of doing it, and consequently they get their own sound going.

"They call it rhythm-and-blues, but it's not the same as what I know as rhythm-and-blues. When I was doing R&B in 1948, and around then, there were only Negro singers doing it.

"Then when Elvis Presley came out and sold well, someone coined the name rock'n'roll. I mean, they couldn't call his music rhythm-and-blues because the Negro was singing R&B.

"Now, among your singers that I've heard, that singer with the Rolling Stones—I don't know his name—gets closest to the blues. He's got a feel . . . he's in the right direction."

ACTING

"My own view on blues is this: you sing what you know, what you are, what you have lived. That way it sounds true. I mean, take John Lee Hooker, who was over here recently.

"He sings about what he's lived through, and what he feels, and he sings the way he talks. Have you noticed that about blues singers? They sing the way they talk, and talk the way they sing.

"It's a drag that most of the kids here get their image of blues only from the folk singer, or so-called country blues.

"Number one: that's why they don't care nothing about dressing.

Above: Although not in the front line of household-name blues singers, Jimmy exerted considerable influence on the British blues bands of the 60s.

And number two: they only know the country singers. If you asked them, they'd know nothing about the king—Joe Turner.

"And the other thing is that word 'soul.' It's misused; it isn't a type of music, it's a quality in the performance. It's got to come from you, you and the musicians, and you don't know when it's going to happen.

"You can sing or play all night and not get it.

"Ben Webster taught me that. And he taught me this also: that time is the greatest thing in the world."

Earlier, on his first UK visit, Jimmy had spoken with Max Jones.

I'VE BEEN LUCKY WITH MY TENORS

"This is my first time in Britain, professionally speaking, and I have to say it's been the best three weeks in my whole career, all the way round.

"It's been better even than my European tour with Buck Clayton in 1961. And that was a good one, and I visited a lot of places. Here, it's been great reactions everywhere.

"Working with Ronnie's group has been a ball. I like to sing with anybody who knows what he's doing, and those guys do. Ronnie himself is beautiful. I told him I'd been lucky with tenor players.

"I just worked with Ben Webster for a long while, and then I sang with Coleman Hawkins. Now I'm working with Ronnie Scott. You know, he does 'Gee Baby' with me, and I had him play another chorus and a half because he did it so beautifully.

"Very few of the young players can play that kind of music. They have to have a little grits, you know. They have to have paid a little dues.

"The rhythm's good, too. I play around with the time a lot, but it doesn't throw them. Now Stan Tracey . . . this man knows what he's doing. He played some introductions the other night that were nobody's business.

"Of course, now and again he'll play one of those pregnant eighths. I call him the English Monk.

"Speaking about the groups I've worked with, I must say that I enjoyed singing with Chris Barber.

"I liked Barber's band. It was a little more modern than the Wilbur de Paris group, and they sure did play for me.

"That trumpet man, Pat Halcox, he played very nicely behind me on the slow tunes.

"While I'm on bands that make you work, Basie's band will drive you. I went to Japan last year with them, and Bill asked me to come to England. But my wife, Diane, was expecting a baby so I had to say 'no.'

"I love Basie. That man's such a giant, and he's the greatest tempo man in the world. Usually, I stomp off the tempo to make sure it's right. I did that first night with Basie, then next day I told him: 'You got it.'

"Now about the blues, and my singing. I sing the blues, but I can sing with a jazz group . . . I can work with anybody.

"I credit this to my apprenticeship with Jay McShann. He's the one who first taught me to play around with the melody and the time.

"I don't sing country blues, of course, but I like some of it. I mean, it is basically good music, though I don't go along with everything those singers do. I like to sing in meter.

"One more point I must make. They keep bringing these country singers and players over here, and the kids think this is the real thing, the typical Negro blues. That's where they're wrong; it isn't."

Below: Jimmy on stage with the British tenor sax star—and famed jazz club proprietor—Ronnie Scott. The blues singer appeared at Ronnie's club several times during his career.

159

Above: Witherspoon in the early 60s—his music career followed a somewhat erratic pattern in terms of the ups and downs of fame.

key recordings

1949	After replacing Walter Brown in the Jay McShann band, Witherspoon has his first R&B hit with *"Ain't Nobody's Business."*
1949-52	More hits on Supreme and Modern with McShann are later collected on Black Lion and RCA compilations.
1959	The near legendary Monterey Jazz Festival set was captured and later issued on *"Rockin' with Spoon,"* where it is combined with an equally satisfying set recorded at the Renaissance Club in Los Angeles from the same year, with Ben Webster and Gerry Mulligan.
1959	*"Spoon Concerts"* LP featuring Webster, Hawkins, Eldridge, et al.
1965	*"Some of My Best Friends Are the Blues"* LP with horn and string arrangements by Benny Golson. The title track was released as a single but it was the flipside *"You're Next,"* which became the Top 100 hit.
1969	*"With Junior Mance"* teamed Spoon with the pianist in a live setting recorded in France, reissued as CD in 1997 on Stony Plain label.
1970	*"Blues Singer"* with UK R&B star Eric Burdon.
1975	Featured on Jon Hendrick's *"Evolution of the Blues Song"* LP on Columbia.
1975	*"Love Is a Five Letter Word"* on Capitol settles in the Top 200.
1979-80	*"Jimmy Witherspoon and Panama Francis' Savoy Sultans"* LP features Spoon in company with trumpeter Irv Stokes and an organ trio reworking Jimmy Rushing covers and other crowd-pleasers.
1980	*"Sings the Blues"* with the Savoy Sultans.
1981	*"Big Blues"* LP recorded in London and released on JSP.
1989	*"Meets the Jazz Giants"* LP recorded in 1959 released on JSP.
1992	*"The Blues, the Whole Blues, and Nothin' but the Blues"* LP.

160 acknowledgments

Front Cover Christian Him's Jazz Index/Tim Motion. ***Back Cover*** Hulton Getty Picture Collection. ***Front Endpaper*** Redferns/Bob Willoughby. ***Back Endpaper*** The Special Photographers Library/Herman Leonard. *p.1* Redferns/Michael Ochs Archives. *p.2-3* Rex Features. *p.4-5* Top Redferns/Michael Ochs Archives. *p.6-7* The Special Photographers Library/Tim Motion. *p.8-9* Redferns/David Redfern. *p.10-11* The Special Photographers Library/Herman Leonard. *p.13* Corbis UK Ltd/UPI/Bettmann. *p.14* Corbis UK Ltd. *p.16* Redferns/ William Gottlieb/Library of Congress. *p.18* Redferns/David Redfern. *p.19* left Corbis UK Ltd/UPI/Bettman. *p.19* right Val Wilmer. *p.20* Hulton Getty Picture Collection/Haywood Magee. *p.21* Redferns/David Redfern. *p.22* Christian Him's Jazz Index/The Peter Vacher Collection. *p.23* Redferns/William Gottlieb/Library of Congress. *p.24* The Special Photographers Library/William Claxton. *p.26* Redferns/Bob Willoughby. *p.27* Top The Special Photographers Library/William Claxton. *p.27* Bottom The Special Photographers Library/William Claxton. *p.28* The Special Photographers Library/William Claxton. *p.29* The Special Photographers Library/William Claxton. *p.30* Redferns/Bob Willoughby. *p.31* The Special Photographers Library/William Claxton. *p.32* The Special Photographers Library/Herman Leonard. *p.34* Redferns/David Redfern. *p.35* Rex Features. *p.36* left Rex Features. *p.36* right Redferns/Michael Ochs Archives. *p.37* Redferns/David Redfern. *p.38* right Rex Features/Dezo Hoffman. *p.38* Centre Rex Features. *p.39* Rex Features. *p.40* Val Wilmer. *p.42* Val Wilmer. *p.43* Christian Him's Jazz Index/The Peter Vacher Collection. *p.44* Bottom Redferns/Michael Ochs Archives. *p.44-45* Top Rex Features. *p.45* Corbis UK Ltd/UPI/ Bettmann. *p.46* The Special Photographers Library/William Claxton. *p.47* Redferns/David Redfern. *p.48-49* Redferns/William Gottlieb/ Library of Congress. *p.50* Redferns/Michael Ochs Archives. *p.51* Redferns/William Gottlieb. *p.52* Redferns/Bob Willoughby. *p.53* Redferns/Bob Willoughby. *p.55* Redferns/Michael Ochs Archives. *p.56* Redferns/Michael Ochs Archives. *p.57* Corbis UK Ltd/UPI/Bettmann. *p.58* The Special Photographers Library/Ronny Jaques. *p.59* Redferns/Chuck Stewart. *p.60* Hulton Getty Picture Collection. *p.61* Redferns/William Gottlieb/Library Of Congress. *p.62-63* The Special Photographers Library/Herman Leonard. *p.64* Corbis UK Ltd/UPI/Bettmann. *p.65* Redferns/Bob Willoughby. *p.66* Corbis UK Ltd/Bettmann. *p.67* Redferns/William Gottlieb/Library Of Congress. *p.68* Corbis UK Ltd/Pittsburgh Courier/ Charles Harris. *p.68-69* Corbis UK Ltd/Pittsburgh Courier/ Charles Harris. *p.70-71* The Special Photographers Library/Herman Leonard. *p.72* right Redferns/David Redfern. *p.72* Centre Corbis UK Ltd/Bettmann. *p.73* Redferns/ David Redfern. *p.74* The Special Photographers Library/Herman Leonard. *p.75* right Corbis UK Ltd/Hulton Deutsch Collection. *p.76* Corbis UK Ltd/Bettmann. *p.77* Redferns/Max Jones Files. *p.78-79* Redferns/Michael Ochs Archives. *p.80* Redferns/Michael Ochs Archives. *p.81* Redferns/William Gottlieb. *p.82* Redferns/Bob Willoughby. *p.83* left The Special Photographers Library/Ronny Jaques. *p.83* right Corbis UK Ltd. *p.84* The Special Photographers Library/Herman Leonard. *p.85* Redferns/William Gottlieb/ Library Of Congress. *p.86-87* Redferns/Bob Willoughby. *p.88* left Redferns/Michael Ochs Archives. *p.89* Redferns/Michael Ochs Archives. *p.90* left Redferns/Bob Willoughby. *p.90* right Corbis UK Ltd/ Hulton Deutsch Collection. *p.91* Rex Features. *p.93* The Special Photographers Library/William Claxton. *p.94* left Redferns/David Redfern. *p.94* right Val Wilmer. *p.95* The Special Photographers Library/Herman Leonard. *p.96* The Special Photographers Library/Herman Leonard. *p.97* The Special Photographers Library/Herman Leonard. *p.98* Val Wilmer. *p.100* left Redferns/David Redfern. *p.100* right Redferns/Brian Shuel. *p.101* Val Wilmer. *p.102* Christian Him's Jazz Index/Jak Kilby. *p.103* Redferns/David Redfern. *p.104* Redferns/ David Redfern. *p.106* Redferns/David Redfern. *p.107* Redferns/David Redfern. *p.108-109* Rex Features. *p.109* right Redferns/David Redfern. *p.110* Redferns/David Redfern. *p.111* Rex Features/Dezo Hoffman. *p.112* Redferns/Bob Willoughby. *p.114* Redferns/Bob Willoughby. *p.115* Redferns/William Gottlieb. *p.116* Redferns/Bob Willoughby. *p.117* Hulton Getty Picture Collection/Ronald Startup. *p.118* Redferns/William Gottlieb. *p.119* Redferns/Bob Willoughby. *p.120* Redferns/Michael Ochs Archives. *p.122* Rex Features. *p.123* The Special Photographers Library/William Claxton. *p.124* Val Wilmer. *p.125* left Corbis UK Ltd/Hulton Deutsch Collection. *p.126* Christian Him's Jazz Index/John Hopkins. *p.127* Christian Him's Jazz Index/John Hopkins. *p.129* Val Wilmer. *p.130* Top Val Wilmer. *p.130* Bottom Left Christian Him's Jazz Index. *p.131* Christian Him's Jazz Index/Mike Doyle. *p.132* left Christian Him's Jazz Index/Mike Doyle. *p.132* right Val Wilmer. *p.133* Val Wilmer. *p.135* The Special Photographers Library/Herman Leonard. *p.136* The Special Photographers Library/Herman Leonard. *p.137* left The Special Photographers Library/Herman Leonard. *p.137* right Redferns/Chuck Stewart. *p.138* Redferns/Michael Ochs Archives. *p.138* right Redferns/William Gottlieb/ Library of Congress. *p.139* Redferns/Max Jones Files. *p.140* Redferns/Max Jones Files. *p.141* right The Special Photographers Library/Herman Leonard. *p.143* The Special Photographers Library/Herman Leonard. *p.144* Redferns/Michael Ochs Archives. *p.145* The Special Photographers Library/William Claxton. *p.146* Redferns/ Chuck Stewart. *p.147* The Special Photographers Library/Herman Leonard. *p.148-149* The Special Photographers Library/Tim Motion. *p.150* The Special Photographers Library/ Herman Leonard. *p.151* The Special Photographers Library/Herman Leonard. *p.152* Redferns. *p.153* Redferns/David Redfern. *p.154* Val Wilmer. *p.156* Christian Him's Jazz Index/Tim Motion. *p.157* left Christian Him's Jazz Index/Tim Motion. *p.157* right Redferns/Michael Ochs Archives. *p.158* Rex Features/Dezo Hoffman. *p.159* Redferns/Michael Ochs Archives.